Functional Writing

Functional Writing

A. D. Van Nostrand   *Brown University*

C. H. Knoblauch   *Columbia University*

Peter J. McGuire   *Georgia Institute of Technology*

Joan Pettigrew   *Center for Research in Writing, Rhode Island*

Houghton Mifflin Company   ·   Boston   *Dallas   Geneva, Ill.   Hopewell, N.J.   Palo Alto   London*

Printed in the U.S.A.

Library of Congress Catalog Card Number: 77-074098

ISBN: 0-395-25294-6

Contents

Part 4 Completing the Argument   295

Preface

Functional Writing is a text/workbook that analyzes the writing process. It is descriptive, not prescriptive. It shows the writer certain mental operations that are common to all writing, and it illustrates ways of controlling these operations to suit the writer's purpose. These operations are choices that the writer makes in deriving relationships from any set of information and are also choices in selecting new information to support those relationships. The writing process is dynamic and repetitive. The writer generates knowledge by writing.

This book presents the learner with ways of controlling these choices. It describes choices in terms of making assertions, of selecting evidence from sets of information, of inferring a reader's frame of reference, and of using that frame of reference to guide the development of the writer's own organizing idea. *Functional Writing* explains the necessary tension between one's natural groping for something to say and the need to say it in a way that a reader can comprehend. Specifically, this book shows the writer how to use a reader's expectations as a means of guiding the writer's choices.

Functional Writing is also a system of instruction that reinforces the instructor's primary task, which is the evaluation of writing. Coordinated with each of the mental operations it describes, the text presents a precise definition of standards for evaluating the writer's work. These standards are stated in seven major structural terms, without reference to subject or to what is often called "content." These structural terms can be referred to any writing sample. Accordingly, the system makes it possible for both the learner and the instructor to speak the same language when they analyze any written statement.

The text is sequential and cumulative. Every chapter appears in the same format. The book can be used alone or with other instructional material, including texts for reading, style manuals, and handbooks for editing. Because the text is sequential, the student can sustain interruptions without having to retrace previous assignments. Because the workbook sections are cumulative, the learner can readily transfer what he or she learns at any stage to other writing activities in other subjects.

Functional Writing presents small units of instruction that are based on the concept of mastery learning. It is therefore possible for instructors to adapt the pace of instruction to learners who start at different levels of achievement. The adaptability of this text was developed through extensive field testing. During five years, the book was used and evaluated at fifteen sites, including two-year colleges, four-year colleges, and technical institutes. It was used in classrooms and in language laboratories, and students who worked with it represented all levels from grade twelve through graduate courses. The text was stored in a computer and revised periodically in accordance with responses from instructors and from students.

Functional Writing was developed under the auspices of The Center for Research in Writing. During the process of adapting a theory of rhetoric to a format for individualized study, the authors received extensive help from The Center for Personalized Instruction at Georgetown University. During the early phases of field testing and again during the testing of an instructor's manual, this writing project received timely assistance from the Exxon Education Foundation. The authors are grateful for this help and support; we trust that *Functional Writing* is a more effective learning instrument as a result of it.

A.D.V.
C.H.K.
P.J. McG.
J.P.

Functional Writing

Introduction

1. A Forecast of the Text

Functional Writing makes several assumptions about anyone who might read it. The first assumption is that you want to write what you mean in a way that enables your intended reader to understand it. Presumably you want to do this as quickly and easily as possible.

A second assumption is that you find it harder to write something than to say it. This is a normal response because writing is more deliberate than speaking. It presents you with different options for saying precisely what you mean. This book will show you how to use those options to define more exactly what you want to communicate when you write.

A third assumption is that you want to apply what you learn about writing to any statement you are committed to write. Presumably the sooner you can do this the better. That statement might be an exam, or a term paper, or a lab report. It might be a letter to the editor or the minutes of a meeting. It might be a list of complicated instructions, a memo to the head of your department, or a magazine article. In any case, you want to apply whatever you learn to any and all functional writing that you may undertake.

In view of these assumptions, you can expect certain things from this book. You can expect to learn how to achieve your purpose in any functional writing, no matter how much or how little you have written. Specifically, you can expect to gain control of your natural habits as a writer. This book will give you a chance to exercise those habits until you can accomplish your purpose every time you write.

What Is Writing?

Writing is a process. As you will see, it is a process of making and stating relationships. It seems reasonable that the more you know about this process the better you can control it. Specifically, the more you know about the way to make choices when you write, the better you can make those choices suit your purpose.

This book will present you with many choices to make. You will be able to make them in the context of exact and limited writing situations. The book will present these choices in a way that will enable you to see what you are doing as you do it. The strategy of *Functional Writing* is to show you how to analyze what you write as you are writing. If you can make this kind of analysis, you will find it relatively easy to modify any statement as you are writing it.

The book will show you how to analyze what you write by slowing down the process that you go through, and by raising questions about what you are doing as you do it. Beginning with the next chapter you will have some elemental choices to make as you proceed through the text. The choices themselves do not become more difficult, but they accumulate as you proceed through the text. In later chapters you will have more choices to coordinate.

Meantime, here are some questions. Your answering these questions will illustrate how this book functions, that is, how it slows down the process of making choices so that you can analyze it.

1. What is the first assumption of this book?

2. What control can you expect to gain from this book?

3. What kind of analysis will this book help you to make?

4. As you proceed through this text, why will your choice-making become more complex?

The Sequence of the Book

Functional Writing is presented in four parts. Each part contains a group of chapters that deal with some important aspect of the writing process. The four parts are sequential and cumulative.

Part 1, called "Making Relationships," describes and illustrates the natural exploratory process that takes place when you write. Searching for relationships is the essence of any writing. What you communicate to your reader is the set of relationships you have found among pieces of information relevant to your subject. The chapters in Part 1 concentrate on the way you make these connections by writing.

Part 2, called "Writing to Readers," describes and illustrates the needs and expectations of all readers. You learn about their frames of reference in order to discover how to communicate. The chapters in Part 2 will show you how to use an intended reader's expectations to your own advantage, and to the reader's advantage as well.

All readers, of course, are different, and every reader has a unique frame of reference that you must accommodate if that reader is to understand what you are saying. On the other hand, all readers have certain traits in common. Your awareness of these traits will guide you in choosing the information you need to support yur purpose. Accordingly, these chapters describe the traits of the Common Reader and show you how to use them to anticipate questions that any intended reader is likely to ask about your statement.

By anticipating the reader's questions the writer can more easily select and organize information, whether in a sentence, a paragraph, or a sequence of paragraphs. In all of these contexts the writer's strategies for conveying information are based on the reader's expectations. Accordingly, in Part 3 you will learn how to arrange assertions in sequences that accommodate your reader's expectations.

Part 3 will also show you how to forecast the sequence that you intend. One illustration of forecasting is the chapter you are now reading. It is describing the organizing ideas of this book and predicting the sequence in which they will occur.

There is still more to building an argument. Later chapters in Part 3 will show you how to expand an argument as you write; that is, they will show you how to generate new relationships and make new assertions while still accommodating the reader. They will also show you how to keep the reader continually informed of the changes you are making as you write.

Part 4 of *Functional Writing* is called "Completing the Argument." The chapters of Part 4 develop all of the operations you have been learning. They show you how to complete your argument with a conclusion that represents your full discovery of what you wanted to say. The most important achievement in writing is your conclusion. In fact, the conclusion is your reason for writing. It fulfills your promise to your intended reader to say something significant. It also completes your process of learning about some subject.

Part 4 ends with the description of a Functional Writing Model. This model incorporates all the concepts that have been introduced in earlier chapters. It represents those concepts as an integrated process. Specifically, the model explains how the interdependent relationship between yourself and your reader leads you to explore your subject completely and to communicate your argument effectively.

According to the Functional Writing Model, any writer offers a contract to some intended reader; that is, the writer offers information in return for the reader's attention. The reader enters into this contract expecting to receive something useful. The writer's concern, therefore, is to fulfill the contract by making choices in writing that acknowledge the reader's expectations. For this purpose the reader's questions are the writer's best guidelines. Accordingly, the Contract Theory of Writing can be stated in one sentence:

> It is easier to organize your information
> for someone else
> than it is to organize it for yourself.

Functional Writing will show you how to implement the theory in any statement that you wish to write. It will show you how to anticipate the reader's needs, how to translate these needs into simple questions, and how to incorporate these questions in your own writing process.

As you work through successive chapters of *Functional Writing*, the concepts it presents should become clearer to you. You will see that they all relate to your own habits when you write. Knowing the concepts will enable you to control your writing habits better than you could before. You will write more coherently in less time than it now takes. That is the promise this book makes in return for your attention. By mastering the information in each successive chapter, and by practicing the operations that you learn, you can fulfill that promise for yourself.

Here are some more questions. Answering them will help you anticipate your experience with this book.

1. As indicated in the description of Part 1, what search is the essence of the writing process?

2. As indicated in the description of Part 2, what can you use to your own advantage and also to the reader's advantage?

3. What will Part 3 show you about expanding an argument?

4. As indicated in the description of Part 4, what does a conclusion represent?

5. State the Contract Theory of Writing.

Part 1: Making Relationships

2. The Nature of Assertions

Writing is a learning process. When you write you learn about your subject; that is, you discover relationships among the pieces of information you have gathered for the statement you will write. No matter what your subject is or how much you already know about it, your writing causes you to learn more about it as you go along.

Writing is also a way to communicate. You can communicate only when you find some connection among your pieces of information. You communicate by making assertions about those connections, not by naming a subject. Writing consists of asserting relationships among pieces of information. You start with a subject, but the subject is not very helpful once you begin to write. You move beyond it as soon as you find your first relationship.

What Is a Subject?

A subject is that part of your environment on which you are concentrating at any moment. This environment could include what you know and experience and remember. When you focus on a given aspect of your environment, for example, economics or bowling or the weather, you have a subject. Your subject establishes the boundaries within which you search for information to include in your statement.

13

"Information" is a basic concept here. In common usage, "information" is a collective word that simply means "data." More precisely, "information" is used here to indicate those data stored in your memory that you retrieve in order to communicate. Accordingly, what you characteristically write down as notes are pieces of information. They are sometimes sentences, but more commonly fragments, that is, words or phrases. These fragments are susceptible to relationship: they can be connected together.

Given any subject, you select pieces of information that relate to it, at the same time excluding other pieces of information. Choices about what to say are guided and restricted by the limits of your subject.

If the subject is "space exploration," for example, you might select information about space satellites, astronauts, rocket fuels, or even Flash Gordon. At the same time, you would probably reject information about agriculture, nineteenth-century literature, or folk songs. Your subject shows you where to look for information: it focuses your attention, thereby simplifying your search for the raw materials of your statement.

The usefulness of a subject by itself can be overestimated. Books about writing characteristically begin with a chapter about "discovering your subject." This book does not—for a good reason: a subject is inert. You can name it, but the name by itself conveys almost no significance. You begin to see what is significant about your subject only when you begin to find relationships among the pieces of information that you have selected.

Finding Relationships

Discovering connections among things is at the heart of the learning process. You understand separate ideas or concepts by associating them with other concepts to form systems of information. Each time you discover how one concept connects with another, you are learning something new. By discovering such a connection, you expand your understanding of the concepts you started with, and you also derive a new concept that relates them.

You already recognize certain conventional modes of relationship. Relating by classes is the most familiar, whereby things are connected on the basis of characteristics they share. The dragon, the unicorn, and the centaur are all mythological beasts. The term "mythological beasts" signifies the class to which these creatures belong; this term denotes a class or category of relationship.

Causal connection is another familiar way of making relationships. The concepts "mosquito" and "malaria" can be related causally since some types of mosquito transmit malaria. A causal connection is implicit in the expression, "where there's smoke there's fire."

A third familiar mode of relationship is hierarchy. A hierarchy is an arrangement of pieces of information in a series, proceeding either in increasing order or decreasing order. The concepts "cardinal," "bishop," and "priest," for example, are related according to an order of rank. These concepts could also be related by class, since each concept denotes a type of Catholic clergyman. There are often several ways of relating the same information.

Conventional modes of relationship comprise only a small fraction of the relationships that you continually make. Finding relationships is a natural habit: it is the essence of your natural learning process. You do it instinctively every time you look at the world around you. Writing is simply one form of that learning process: it causes you to make connections among ideas. When you make connections, you perceive that your information has a new significance. That new significance is what you communicate.

An Example of Making Relationships

Suppose your subject is "the ocean" and you want to write a statement about it. Your statement could be a sentence, or a paragraph, or a book; it could be a discourse of any length. Suppose you have collected some information about this subject that you want to communicate. The pieces of information would be various: some might be specific and some might be general. But your notes, simplified, might include the following:

- sea plants
- waves and tides
- types of fish
- temperature of currents
- the ocean floor
- marine biology

This list presents a problem typical of any writing situation. You have a subject and a collection of information, but you have not yet discovered what you want to say. Merely knowing your subject does not help very much. Moreover, the information is not automatically arranged merely because it falls within the limits of the subject. Your problem is to find a way of associating separate concepts in order to make a pattern of those concepts. There are many different relationships that you could make using these pieces of information about the ocean.

Look again at the information. Suppose you relate environmental factors to the locations of different schools of fish. You might state the relationship this way:

> Various features of the ocean environment determine where different species of fish live.

This sentence asserts a relationship among the pieces of information. It represents what you are learning about your subject, which is what you are communicating.

You communicate a relationship by making an assertion about it. An assertion is any declaration about a relationship or about a number of relationships. By declaring a relationship, you assert the significance of the information you relate; that is, you show how it all fits together: you show how one piece supports or clarifies another. Therefore, making an assertion about any information is the same as stating the significance of that information.

Notice that the assertion about the ocean is expressed as a sentence. There is a reason for this. In writing, a sentence is the shortest written statement that conveys an assertion about a relationship. Words or phrases convey only subjects: "the yellow pages," or "up a tree," or "running along the road." But what about those yellow pages or that tree or that road? You cannot make an assertion about any of these subjects in less than a sentence.

An Example of Making Assertions

Again, suppose the subject is "the ocean." The following information all pertains to this subject. See if a possible relationship occurs to you as you read through the information in the list. Any relationship you find will help provide you with a strategy for associating all the pieces of information in some pattern.

- value of coastal waters
- minerals can be obtained from the ocean
- national control of coastlines
- sharing ocean resources
- the full potential of the ocean floor
- the ocean as a food source

One first impression might be that there is some connection between nations and food resources. This impression is indefinite to begin with. Through the process of writing, however, the writer would discover the significance of that relationship. For example, the writer might assert: "Ocean resources must be shared by all nations." This assertion connects all the information in the list. Now look at a paragraph that makes these connections explicit:

> Throughout history, the coastal *nations have considered their shorelines exclusive property.* However, as other nations become aware of *the potential wealth available in coastal waters,* this assumption is being challenged. Even landlocked nations have learned that much of *their population can be fed* from the *coastal fisheries* and that *raw materials that are now being taken from the ocean floor* can replace their own dwindling natural resources. As these nations come to realize that their continued prosperity depends on their access to ocean resources, they are demanding *a share in these resources.* The coastal nations must either meet this demand or face years of strife.

Notice that the sentences in this paragraph do not literally repeat all the information in the list. The connections do not depend on the actual words but on the concepts that they represent to the writer. Words are labels. Connections are not inherent in the words themselves but in the associations that the writer perceives. The relationships are logical, not merely grammatical. There are many other assertions that you might state using the same set of information. Someone else might assert, for example: "Control of coastlines guarantees a nation an exclusive right to ocean resources." Had you chosen this assertion, you would probably develop your paragraph differently.

Summary

Writing is a learning process. As you begin to think about your subject, you gather pieces of information about it. As you select pieces of information, you make connections among them. Gathering and connecting pieces of information cause you to learn about your subject. The connections that you make are what you communicate, and you communicate them in the form of assertions: that is, in sentences that declare relationships. These statements of relationship reveal the significance of your information.

Name _____ Instructor _____ _____

Do You Understand the Concept of Making Assertions?

The following questions will aid you in summarizing what you have learned in this chapter.

How does your subject help you as a writer?

Why does a subject by itself not enable you to organize and communicate information?

What do you search for when you write?

Check the right answer. In writing you discover what you want to say when:

a. you accumulate a list of information or a set of concepts
b. you make a relationship that connects the items in a list of information

What do you have to do to communicate a relationship?

What is an assertion?

Why must an assertion be expressed as a sentence?

How do you assert the significance of your information?

Now Make Some Assertions of Your Own

Working through the following writing situations will demonstrate your mastery of this chapter. Your instructor may suggest other situations or may encourage you to create your own.

Given any set of information pertaining to a subject, you should be able to assert a relationship that associates the information in a pattern.

Read through the lists of information below. What patterns do the pieces of information in each list suggest to you? Think of a way to relate the pieces of information in each list. Use your imagination freely. There are many possible relationships in any set of information. You alone are responsible for discovering the significance of your raw materials in any writing situation.

For each list of information:

1. Select at least four items.
2. Find a relationship among these items and assert it in the space provided.
3. Write a paragraph that organizes all the information in terms of the relationship you have discovered.

Subject:
   on safari

List of Information:
- antelopes stampeding across the plain
- flies abound in the marshland
- the kick of an elephant gun
- freedom and danger
- lush, dense greenery and tropic heat

State a possible assertion in one sentence:

Name _____ Instructor _____

Write a paragraph that expresses the relationship you have asserted and that uses all the information:

Subject:
   television in the United States

List of Information:

- silence is golden
- American entertainment standards
- enjoyment of whatever you like
- the usefulness of educational television
- the new opiate of the masses

State a possible assertion in one sentence:

Name _____ Instructor_____

Write a paragraph that expresses the relationship you have asserted and that uses all the information:

Subject:
   mass transit

List of Information:

- □ cities and the use of automobiles
- □ the cost of new highways
- □ suburbs must share the cost
- □ cars and personal freedom
- □ a matter of politics

State a possible assertion in one sentence:

Name ———————————————— Instructor————————————————

Write a paragraph that expresses the relationship you have asserted and that uses all the information:

3. The Writer's Organizing Idea

Chapter 2 stated that an assertion is a declaration of the relationships you have made among pieces of information. An assertion declares the significance of that information.

This chapter focuses on the process of organizing a statement. As you begin to write, you make an estimate of what you want to say. This estimate is a tentative organizing idea. It may be the first assertion that comes to mind, or it may be the one you select from several that occur to you. In any case, this tentative organizing idea will evolve as you write.

The Writer's Tentative Organizing Idea

Suppose your favorite team has lost an important game for what you think are all the wrong reasons. You decide to write a letter to the local sports editor expressing your reaction: "Losing the game wasn't our team's fault. There were many reasons that had nothing to do with the way they played." These are already tentative assertions about the game's outcome.

The first step in writing your letter to the editor would probably involve thinking about the game and trying to decide why you felt as you did about it. If you made notes, they might look like this:

- officiating
- terrible weather
- game played on opponent's field

- crowd noise constantly interfered with our team's signal calling
- inexperienced players get distracted

Notice that the first three items on the list, "officiating," "terrible weather," and "played on opponent's field," are all information fragments. As stated in Chapter 2, these pieces of information by themselves convey almost no significance. As a writer you must discover the significance of these fragments and make an assertion that states it.

The two other items on the list are already assertions: "crowd noise constantly interfered with our team's signal calling" and "inexperienced players get distracted." If you decide to include these assertions in your letter, then you must relate them to the information fragments. You need to incorporate all the items in your statement. You can incorporate the items by making a tentative assertion: "The team's loss was due to many factors not directly related to the quality of play." You can then use this assertion as an organizing idea.

What Is an Organizing Idea?

An organizing idea is an assertion that relates the information in any paragraph or sequence of paragraphs. It is your declaration about the significance of your information. It is the most important assertion you make in any statement. Finding an organizing idea is your primary task as you write, and it is also your reason for writing. As you evaluate your information, you search for an organizing idea to hold it together.

An organizing idea develops from your effort to relate the pieces of information you include in your statement. It is an assertion you formulate in your own mind; it is not inherent in the information itself or in any property of the information. An organizing idea depends solely on the way you see the information.

In traditional rhetoric, the organizing idea in a paragraph is often called a "topic sentence." Although any good paragraph contains some organizing principle, not all paragraphs contain topic sentences. "Organizing idea," therefore, is a more accurate term for the principle of relationship in writing because it is not limited to being explicit. An organizing idea may actually occur as one of the sentences in a paragraph or in a series of paragraphs, or it may be implied by the other assertions that you make. An organizing idea is inherent in the logic of any good paragraph or sequence of paragraphs, but it does not have to be explicitly stated.

Unlike a topic sentence, an organizing idea is not static. It begins in your consciousness as an impression of the probable connections you will establish. This impression is tentative; it is your best estimate of the significance of your information. It grows progressively clearer to you as you write. You come to recognize your developed organizing idea only through your effort to evolve a logical statement. The concept of topic sentence denies the possibility of growth or development. It assumes that a writer has already found a fully evolved idea. But in most paragraphs this knowledge is an achievement of the writing process, not a ready-made conclusion at the start.

Look back at the set of information about the game. There are many possible organizing ideas for the information you have collected for your letter to the sports editor. One could be: "Poor officiating and physical factors caused the loss." Another might be: "Our team lost because it lacked experience." Still other organizing ideas are possible, either explicit or implied.

To summarize:

- An organizing idea is an assertion you formulate in your own mind.
- It begins as an estimate of the significance of your information and develops as you write.
- It is an assertion that will enable you to relate the information in your statement.
- It is a logical component of your finished statement, whether or not it actually occurs as a sentence.

How Does an Organizing Idea Function?

Notice that the tentative organizing ideas for the letter to the sports editor are expressed as sentences, not merely as words or phrases. Chapter 2 explained that an assertion must be expressed as a sentence because a sentence is the shortest written statement that asserts a relationship. An organizing idea is an assertion. Therefore, if it is an explicit assertion, it takes the form of a sentence. If it is an implicit assertion, it should be readily convertible to the form of a sentence.

Statements of more than a sentence (whether a paragraph or a sequence of paragraphs) normally convey many assertions. If the subject is "the Peloponnesian War," for example, a paragraph or paragraph sequence related to that subject would make many assertions about it. One of these assertions would be the organizing idea: that is, the most important assertion in the paragraph or paragraph sequence. The other assertions would assist in developing the organizing idea.

In the example of the Peloponnesian War, one organizing idea could be this: "The Peloponnesian War profoundly altered the Greek culture." Another organizing idea might be: "The Peloponnesian War ruined Athens." In each case, the organizing idea would express the essential significance of the paragraph or sequence of paragraphs.

Without an organizing idea the assertions in a statement remain logically unrelated. Here is what can happen when a paragraph lacks an organizing idea. Consider the following collection of sentences about space exploration. The collection masquerades as a paragraph, but do you see why it is not a paragraph?

> Babylonian astronomers were among the first to look at the sky and wonder about the stars. Space satellites have told us much about the physical composition and temperature of many of the planets in our solar system. In Galileo's time, the study of astronomy was called optics, and the first telescopes were crude. Soon unmanned vehicles will land on other planets and conduct scientific experiments.

The statement is unsatisfactory because the four assertions are unrelated to one another. Even though the assertions all fall within the boundaries of the subject, they fail to convey any single significance. In other words, they lack an organizing idea. They cannot be summarized in a sentence.

How an Organizing Idea Relates Information and Assertions in a Paragraph

SUBJECT
   parachuting

SET OF INFORMATION
◻ you would have to be crazy to jump from an airplane
◻ sense of freedom
◻ feeling of transcendence, living at the height of awareness
◻ some people enjoy the experience of danger

TENTATIVE ORGANIZING IDEA
  Parachuting has some strange appeal.

PARAGRAPH
  It seems that you would have to be crazy to jump from an airplane. Yet, skyjumping has appealing aspects. There is a sense of
  freedom that comes from soaring in the air and a feeling of transcendence in escaping the earth's bonds. Also, there is a sense
  of challenge in allowing one's life to depend on the durability
  of a few yards of silk.

DEVELOPED ORGANIZING IDEA
  It would seem that skyjumpers are insane, but the sport is popular
  because it offers freedom, transcendence, and challenge.

Can you see how the writer's tentative organizing idea restates the information? Can you also see how it changes as the paragraph evolves?
This change is represented in the developed organizing idea. In the
beginning, the writer wants to discover why skyjumping is appealing.
The developed organizing idea extends the tentative organizing idea by
stating three reasons why the sport is appealing.
  Now suppose that the writer decides to rewrite. Normally anyone
learns more about a subject by rewriting. The writer can continue to
learn by using the developed organizing idea of the first paragraph as
the tentative organizing idea for rewriting that paragraph.

TENTATIVE ORGANIZING IDEA
(Developed Organizing Idea of the first paragraph)
  It would seem that skyjumpers are insane, but the sport is popular
  because it offers freedom, transcendence, and challenge.

PARAGRAPH
  Leaping from an airplane seems a species of madness. Yet parachuting for sport is growing more popular every day. One reason
  is the sense of freedom that comes from soaring thousands of feet
  in the air. Another reason may be one's feeling of transcendence
  in slipping the surly bonds of earth. But there must also be an un-
  derlying love of danger, a need to live "right at the edge" before
  life can be truly enjoyed, that distinguishes the skyjumper from
  most other sportsmen. It is this fundamental thirst for danger

that pushes the skyjumper out of the door, high above the ground, his life depending on the durability of a few yards of silk.

DEVELOPED ORGANIZING IDEA

The skyjumper is a special breed of sportsman, who values above all else the sense of danger, the special exhilaration associated with his sport.

Can you see how this developed organizing idea represents the writer's most significant assertion? In the second paragraph, the writer has asserted that the third reason, the thirst for danger, is more important than the other two reasons, freedom and transcendence. Rewriting any statement expands your knowledge of your subject. It also sharpens your awareness of your organizing idea.

Summary

You begin to organize your statement as you become aware of the significance of your assertions. When you have discovered a single assertion that relates all the assertions in a paragraph or a sequence of paragraphs, you have a way to organize those assertions. This single assertion is your tentative organizing idea. As you write, it evolves into a developed organizing idea: that is, the most important assertion about your subject.

Do You Understand the Concept of an Organizing Idea?

The following questions will aid you in summarizing what you have learned in this chapter.

Organizing ideas are not inherent in sets of information. Where do they come from?

Sometimes an organizing idea actually occurs in a paragraph as a "topic sentence." But it does not always have to appear as one of the sentences of the paragraph. Why not?

Why must an organizing idea be a sentence rather than a word or a phrase?

What distinguishes an organizing idea from other assertions?

What normally happens to your organizing idea as you write?

Now Put the Concept of Organizing Idea to Work in Your Own Writing

Working through the following writing situations will demonstrate your mastery of this chapter. Your instructor may suggest other situations or may encourage you to create your own.

Given any subject, you should be able to find information, state an organizing idea for that information, and write a paragraph based on that organizing idea.

In the following writing assignments you will have a chance to see how a tentative organizing idea evolves as you write and rewrite. When you have finished each assignment, compare the tentative organizing idea of your original paragraph with your developed organizing idea after rewriting that paragraph.

Select three subjects from the list below:

- the uses of plastic
- slang in the ghetto
- the motorcycle
- pretending
- defense in any team sport
- discipline
- smoking
- the government versus the individual
- vegetarian cooking

For each subject:

a. List four or five pieces of information related to the subject.

b. State a tentative organizing idea.

c. Write a paragraph.

d. State a developed organizing idea.

e. Use the developed organizing idea in rewriting your original paragraph.

f. State a developed organizing idea for your rewritten paragraph.

A. Subject you have selected:

Set of Information:
1.

2.

3.

4.

5.

Tentative Organizing Idea:

Name _____ Instructor _____

Paragraph:

First Developed Organizing Idea:

Paragraph:

Name _____ Instructor_____

Second Developed Organizing Idea:

B. Subject you have selected:

Set of Information:
1.

2.

3.

4.

5.

Tentative Organizing Idea:

Paragraph:

Name _____ Instructor _____

First Developed Organizing Idea:

Paragraph:

Second Developed Organizing Idea:

C. Subject you have selected:

Set of Information:
1.

2.

3.

4.

5.

Name _____ Instructor _____

Tentative Organizing Idea:

Paragraph:

First Developed Organizing Idea:

Paragraph:

Name _____ Instructor_____

Second Developed Organizing Idea:

4. The Writer's Frame of Reference

As you recall from Chapter 3, an organizing idea is an assertion that you formulate in your mind as a means of discovering and communicating a relationship. When you state your organizing idea, you make an assertion about the significance of your information. Another person would probably make a different assertion. There are many possible organizing ideas for any set of information, but all writers derive their organizing ideas from what they believe is significant.

What you think is significant about your information is influenced by your frame of reference, or world view. In the writing process, your frame of reference influences virtually every choice you make in selecting and ordering information.

What Is a Frame of Reference?

Your frame of reference is a composite of your feelings, assumptions, experiences, and values. It is your perspective or world view. Because of their different frames of reference, people respond to the same thing in different ways. (Personality theorists have discussed the origins of a person's frame of reference. This text will discuss frame of reference as it applies to the writing process.)

Consider "the moon" as a subject. To a child the moon may be a face in the sky; to a poet, a symbol; to an astrologer, a sign governing personality. To a primitive man the moon may be a deity; to an astronomer, a body moving through space; to spacecraft engineers, a set of mathematical coordinates. Many other responses are also possible, each determined by the individual's frame of reference.

Your Frame of Reference Influences Your Response to a Subject

A frame of reference is a set of predispositions that could be directed at any number of subjects. Suppose your frame of reference included the belief that reason should prevail over emotion. This perspective could influence your response to many subjects: the American Revolution, romantic love, civil disobedience, self-discipline, or the busing of school children. Your frame of reference always influences the way you react to your information, even though it is rarely explicit in any statement.

It is important to distinguish between "frame of reference" and "organizing idea." An organizing idea is narrower and more defined than a frame of reference. Although a frame of reference can be applied to any number of subjects, a tentative organizing idea applies directly to a single set of information.

See How a Frame of Reference Influences an Organizing Idea

To illustrate how your frame of reference influences your organizing idea, consider how two writers, Smith and Jones, respond to the same subject, "vocational schools." Suppose Smith has this frame of reference: "Social programs should meet everyone's needs." Given this frame of reference, Smith might assert this: "In spite of their higher cost, vocational schools benefit both the student and the economy."

The next task would be to gather more information about the subject. Smith might list this information:

▫ vocational schools train people in usable skills

▫ technicians for industry

- not everyone wants to go to college
- the stigma of attending vocational schools
- vocational schools cost more to operate than traditional high schools

After examining the information, Smith would decide that his or her initial response is supported by the information. Smith's response is now confirmed as a tentative organizing idea, and Smith's statement might look like this:

> It is unfortunate that there is a stigma attached to attending a vocational school. In spite of their high cost of operation, these schools provide at least as much value for each dollar as the academic high school. Vocational schools provide a place for students who do not plan to attend college, and they also train these students in the skills necessary to keep America's industries running.

Suppose Jones has a different frame of reference. Jones believes that social programs are already overemphasizing technology. Given this frame of reference, Jones's response might be: "Tax money should not subsidize vocational schools because that would subsidize industry." After Jones examines the same set of information, he or she would see that this initial response is also a tentative organizing idea. Jones might write a statement that looks like this:

> Not everyone wants to go to college, but that is no reason to spend tax money on costly vocational schools. Vocational programs may be good for industry because they provide technicians, but they are harmful to the students. Although some students think they don't want to go to college, a high school freshman is too young to decide to give up a valuable academic program. He would lose respect in the eyes of his peers by dropping out of high school. If he needs vocational training, he should obtain it after high school and at industry's expense.

You can see that different writers may have different responses to the same subject. Their responses reflect their frames of reference.

Another Example of How a Frame of Reference Influences an Organizing Idea

In any writing situation your frame of reference accounts for the way you see your subject. Your perspective also enables you to organize any information related to that subject. Here is how a frame of reference enables you to discover an organizing idea:

GIVEN THIS FRAME OF REFERENCE
Capitalists always look out for themselves first. Their only interest is profit.

And, THIS SUBJECT
The environment
And, THIS SET OF INFORMATION
- lakes are becoming polluted
- many species of animals are in danger of becoming extinct
- role of government
- provide oxygen
- disposal of industrial waste

HERE IS A TENTATIVE ORGANIZING IDEA: It is the responsibility of government to protect our few remaining wooded areas from destruction by industry.

No matter what your frame of reference might be, the same process of focusing and refining occurs. Here is a different perspective on the same subject. Notice how it yields a different organizing idea.

GIVEN THIS FRAME OF REFERENCE
A country's survival depends on
industry.

And, THIS SUBJECT
The environment
And, THIS SET OF INFORMATION
- lakes are becoming polluted
- many species of animals are
  in danger of becoming extinct
- role of government
- provide oxygen
- disposal of industrial waste

HERE IS A TENTATIVE ORGANIZING
IDEA: Industry must be allowed
to dispose of its waste products,
even if those products damage
the environment.

Notice that in these illustrations each frame of reference is described in a
sentence or two. Much more than a few sentences would be needed to
represent any frame of reference completely, but an organizing idea can
be stated in a single sentence.

Summary

Your frame of reference is a composite of your feelings, assumptions,
experiences, and values. It is your world view, and it may be directed at
any subject. In fact, your frame of reference influences your response to
any subject. But unlike your frame of reference, which can be applied to
many subjects, a tentative organizing idea organizes pieces of information suggested by any given subject.

Can You See the Difference between a Frame of Reference and an Organizing Idea?

The following questions will aid you in summarizing what you have learned in this chapter.

Why do different writers see different organizing ideas in the same set of information?

What is a frame of reference?

How is a frame of reference different from an organizing idea?

Now Put This Knowledge to Use in Your Own Writing

Working through the following writing situations will demonstrate your mastery of this chapter. Your instructor may suggest other situations or may encourage you to create your own.

Given a frame of reference and items of information about a subject, you should be able to state an organizing idea that reflects this frame of reference.

You will notice that the stated frame of reference associated with the following sets 1, 2, 3, and 4 are represented only by a sentence. Remember, however, that these sentences signify only partial perspectives. They are merely convenient labels for a potentially wide range of feelings, assumptions, experiences, and values that constitute any real frame of reference. Hence, you may extend the descriptions of these perspectives any way you like, if it will help you to find an appropriate organizing idea.

A. For all four sets, find an organizing idea and write it in the space provided.

FRAME OF REFERENCE:

SUBJECT:

TENTATIVE ORGANIZING IDEA:

1. Everyone should want to support oneself

liberal arts education
  □ responsibilities of citizenship
  □ making of a whole person
  □ irrelevance
  □ need for technical education
  □ civilization

2. The haves should help the have-nots

world food crises
  □ famine
  □ high cost of fertilizer
  □ overpopulation
  □ problem of food distribution
  □ role of the United Nations

FRAME OF REFERENCE:	SUBJECT:	TENTATIVE ORGANIZING
3. Only culture separates mankind from other animals	liberal arts education □ responsibilities of citizenship □ making of a whole person □ irrelevance □ need for technical education □ civilization	IDEA:
4. People cause their own problems	world food crises □ famine □ high cost of fertilizer □ overpopulation □ problem of food distribution □ role of the United Nations	

B. Choose any one of the previous sets of information and write a paragraph that reflects the frame of reference and the organizing idea you have inferred from the set.

Frame of Reference:

Organizing Idea:

Paragraph:

5. The Nature of Evidence

Earlier chapters in this text emphasized that an organizing idea is an assertion you formulate in your own mind. They also asserted that your frame of reference influences your organizing idea. This chapter discusses the reciprocal relationship between the process of discovering an organizing idea and the process of turning information into evidence.

What Is Evidence?

Writing is a process of turning information into evidence. Information about any subject is available to the writer in great quantity—in fact far greater than necessary. Evidence is only that information which you choose to include in your statement to support your organizing idea. (You will see later that you may use different evidence to support your organizing idea for different readers.) Evidence is anything that helps to clarify or elaborate the organizing idea of a statement. All evidence is information, but all information is not evidence.

There is a reciprocal relationship between the process of discovering an organizing idea and the process of turning information into evidence. The two processes are so closely associated that they often occur simultaneously as you write. Their relationship is this: the more information you collect on a given subject, the more certain you become about the character of your organizing idea; conversely, the more certain you become about your organizing idea, the better you can turn information into evidence that will support it. Here is another way of stating the relationship: searching for information assists you in locating your organizing idea; conversely, discovering your organizing idea assists you in turning information into evidence. Discovering an organizing idea also helps you to reject information that does not support it.

Suppose you are writing a statement on "the abuse of presidential power." You have a frame of reference: individuals are fallible; absolute power should not be placed in the hands of one individual. You normally select information that is consistent with your frame of reference. You are not yet sure of your organizing idea, nor are you certain that all of your information will be useful later. You list your information because you must start somewhere.

Suppose one piece of your information states that localizing power in the presidency is essential to effective government. Another piece of information asserts that the advantages of focusing power in the presidency outweigh the disadvantages. Several examples support these assertions.

You then gather more information. You discover that there are enormous dangers in vesting too much authority in a single individual. You also discover that the more unchecked power a person has, the more egotistical and tyrannical that person is inclined to become. You are already formulating relationships and making assertions. Given your frame of reference and the set of information you have gathered, you begin to see that your most important assertion or tentative organizing idea could be: "Delegating too much power to one individual might turn a representative government into a dictatorship." In other words, as you gather information, you test relationships in an effort to discover your organizing idea.

Suppose you gather two more pieces of information as you write. One states that there are ample constitutional safeguards against a president's abuse of executive authority. Another states that the system of checks and balances written into the Constitution is designed to allow for the free exercise of presidential authority. Gathering information as you write, you grow more certain of the organizing idea you wish to communicate. Your tentative organizing idea has evolved. Now you can make this assertion: "The president should be allowed enough power to enact policy provided the people have the means to check any abuse of that power."

Each of the pieces of information above supports the tentative organizing idea you have discovered. By using this information in your statement and by specifying its connection to your organizing idea, you turn it into evidence. Your information has become evidence because you used it to support or develop your organizing idea. Moreover, your evolving organizing idea now serves to guide you as you search for new evidence.

Suppose you find still more pieces of information. One states that Congress always serves special interest groups more readily than it serves its broader constituency. Another asserts that recent abuses of power point out the need for strengthening national safeguards, but they do not prove the necessity of reducing presidential power.

Could either of these assertions be used as evidence? Clearly, the second piece of information, about recent abuses of power, can be evidence for your statement and should be retained because it supports your organizing idea. But the first piece, about congressional priorities, does not directly support what you want to say, and it should be discarded. It is information, but in this case it is not evidence.

You can tell whether a piece of information is useful as evidence by asking "So what?" or "How does this information clarify or support what I want to say?" While writing about the abuse of presidential power, for example, you might want to ask "So what?" about this assertion: "Only a strong figurehead at the top enables the smooth running of government." You might answer that this information supports your organizing idea because it implies that presidential power should be maintained. You might also question another piece of information, namely, that recent administrations are classic examples of the abuse of presidential power. Your assessment might be that this information also supports your organizing idea. In any case, the question "So what?" will help you to assert the connection between any given piece of information and the organizing idea you are trying to develop.

What about the information that Congress serves special interest groups? So what? Does this information directly relate to your organizing idea about presidential power? Eventually, you might be able to establish some relationship—if you have enough time and enough space to state its connections to the organizing idea in your statement. It is more likely that you would reject it as evidence, however, because it is not immediately relevant to what you want to say. In any case, there is other information already available that more clearly supports your organizing idea.

Potentially any piece of information related to a subject could be turned into evidence for any given organizing idea. But remember: whatever information you select as evidence must clarify and support your organizing idea. If this connection is not clear, then the information is not evidence.

Some pieces of information make better evidence than others; that is, some pieces support or clarify your organizing idea more persuasively than others. You decide the usefulness of a piece of information as evidence by estimating how much time, effort, or space is required to relate it to your organizing idea. Make this decision by comparing the effort expended with the benefit derived. Does the effort exceed the benefit?

Remember these three steps for assessing information as possible evidence:

1. Decide if the piece of information is sufficiently relevant to justify the amount of writing necessary to relate it to your organizing idea.
2. Reject any information that does not meet this test.
3. When you write your statement, be explicit in connecting this relevant information to your organizing idea.

How Evidence Differs from Information

Suppose you are writing a statement about the weather in Minnesota. You feel that warm climates are preferable to cold climates. This frame of reference could produce a response to your subject, "the weather in Minnesota." This response might become a tentative organizing idea: "Minnesota is a terrible place to live in the winter." Which items in the following list of information could serve as evidence for this tentative organizing idea? As you read down the list, cross out the items that would probably not be useful as evidence. This will approximate one kind of choice you make as you write.

1. cold weather, ice, and snow
2. ice-skating
3. driving in snow is dangerous
4. Minnesotans are tougher than Californians
5. I don't like snow

6. Minnesota is located between South Dakota and Wisconsin

7. wind-chill factor

8. winter temperatures in Minnesota can reach 35 degrees below

9. heart attacks from snow shoveling

10. farming state

1. Probable evidence:	It describes the weather in Minnesota and provides a basis for calling the weather uncomfortable.
2. Not evidence:	It would take too long to relate it to the organizing idea and may even contradict it.
3. Probable evidence:	Minnesota has a lot of snow and having to drive in it is hazardous.
4. Not evidence:	It is irrelevant to the organizing idea and probably not true anyway.
5. Probable evidence:	It explains in part the opinion that has given rise to this particular organizing idea.
6. Not evidence:	Although it is true, it is generalized and would probably take too long to include.
7. Probable evidence:	It explains why Minnesota weather is so cold, which is one reason why the weather is miserable in the winter.
8. Probable evidence:	It is proof that Minnesota weather is cold in the winter.
9. Probable evidence:	Snow shoveling may be dangerous.
10. Not evidence:	It neither supports nor clarifies the organizing idea.

Here is one way you might use this evidence to support and clarify your organizing idea:

Minnesota has a lot of cold weather, ice, and snow. The wind-chill factor is acute, and temperatures drop as low as 35 degrees below zero. Freezing weather is bad enough, but the snow that comes with it is even worse. If shoveling the snow out of your driveway doesn't kill you, driving on icy, snow-packed roads probably will.

Another writer with a different frame of reference would write a different statement about Minnesota's weather. For example, if you like winter sports, your opinion might be that Minnesota has the best winter weather in the country.

Summary

Evidence is only that information which supports or clarifies your organizing idea. There is a reciprocal relationship between the process of turning information into evidence and the process of discovering an organizing idea. As you collect more information on a given subject, you become more certain about your organizing idea. As you become more certain of your organizing idea, you can readily convert pieces of information into evidence.

Do You Understand the Concept of Evidence?

The following questions will aid you in summarizing what you have learned in this chapter.

What is evidence and how is it distinguished from information?

What question can you ask to determine whether a piece of information will be useful as evidence? How does asking this question help you to turn information into evidence?

What is the test for deciding whether a particular piece of information is worth including as evidence in a given statement?

What is the reciprocal relationship between discovering an organizing idea and turning information into evidence?

Now Distinguish Evidence from Information in Your Own Writing

Working through the following writing situations will demonstrate your mastery of this chapter. Your instructor may suggest other situations or may encourage you to create your own.

Given any set of information, you should be able to decide which items could serve as evidence for a particular organizing idea; you should also be able to relate any piece of evidence to your organizing idea in a written statement.

Two sets of information related to two different subjects are provided below. For each set:

a. Place a check mark in the appropriate column opposite each item of information, indicating whether or not that item could be evidence.

b. Beneath each item of information, explain your decision to accept or reject it as probable evidence.

Then choose one of the two sets. Write a short statement that incorporates the tentative organizing idea with the evidence you have selected.

SET 1

Frame of Reference:

  Industriousness should be rewarded.

Tentative Organizing Idea:

  I deserve a raise because I qualify for one.

	Probable evidence	Not evidence
Set of Information		
1. You have not talked to the personnel director in a long time.		
2. One of your recent studies has saved the company money.		
3. You enjoy bowling on the company team.		

	Probable evidence	Not evidence

4. In the last three years, you missed one day of work.

5. Another company has offered you a slightly higher salary.

6. You have been a faithful employee for fifteen years.

7. You are married and have two children.

8. The company is hiring many new people.

9. You are working toward a master's degree in business administration.

10. The company has adopted several of your proposals for cutting costs.

SET 2

Frame of Reference:

Protection of the environment is more important than the growth of industry.

Tentative Organizing Idea:

This river is more valuable for recreation than for generating electricity.

	Probable evidence	Not evidence

Set of Information:

1. There is a plan to designate this river as part of our national wilderness.

2. Electricity can be obtained from other sources.

3. Opinion among the citizens is divided.

	Probable evidence	Not evidence

4. Fishing in the river would be reduced.

5. Salmon use the river as a route to spawning areas.

6. The river flows through four states.

7. You have always been opposed to any alteration of the natural environment.

8. Petitions are now being collected to oppose the dam.

9. The river was first seen by settlers in 1759.

Name _____ Instructor_____

	Probable evidence	Not evidence
10. The river is less than twenty-five miles from six large cities.		

Paragraph(s):

6. Review of Part 1

This chapter will serve as a practical review of the concepts you worked with in Part 1: subject, organizing idea, frame of reference, and evidence. You should now be familiar with these concepts, and you should be able to use them when you write.

What Has Part 1 Indicated about Writing?

Writing is a learning process. As you write, you learn by asserting relationships among pieces of information about your subject. Your principal task as you write is to discover your most important assertion: that is, your organizing idea.

There are several concepts that define the nature of the writer's relationship to any information. These concepts are: (1) frame of reference, (2) subject, (3) organizing idea, and (4) evidence. These four concepts are interrelated; their association is represented in the following scheme:

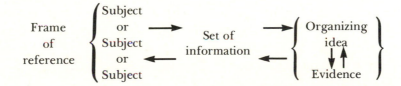

According to this model, your frame of reference exists prior to your choice of any subject; also it influences your choice of information and your choice of an organizing idea.

Your collection of information reflects what you consider important about your subject. It is not the only possible set of information, nor does it exhaust the subject. Other frames of reference can provide other perspectives on the subject and therefore other choices of material.

Sometimes your information takes the form of notes, but just as often it is merely a list. This information becomes evidence only after you have discovered your organizing idea and have asserted how that information supports it. You may discover that you must discard some of your information because it does not qualify as evidence. You may also discover that you need new information to support your organizing idea. As you find information, you develop your tentative organizing idea. As you grow more certain of that organizing idea, you make increasingly more directed choices about how to support it.

Remember the Four Essential Concepts of Part 1

A **subject** is that part of a person's environment on which he or she is focusing attention at any given moment. Writing consists of making assertions about a subject.

Your **frame of reference** is a composite of your feelings, experiences, assumptions, and values. It is a way of viewing the world, a way of responding to the world. This frame of reference partly influences how you regard any subject. Therefore, it influences your choice of an organizing idea.

An **organizing idea** is an assertion of relationship. It is your judgment about the significance of your information; it specifies a pattern or system of relationships. An organizing idea may be implicit or explicit in any paragraph or sequence of paragraphs. It can always be expressed as a sentence that describes or summarizes that paragraph or paragraph sequence.

An organizing idea differs from a subject in this way: a subject establishes boundaries within which you search for information, but an organizing idea is a judgment about relationships among the pieces of information you have selected. Finding a subject helps you to start the process of selecting information. Finding an organizing idea helps you to turn information into evidence.

An organizing idea differs from a frame of reference in this way: a frame of reference governs your responses to any subject on which you might focus your attention. It governs your sense of what is important and what is not important, what is true and what is false, what is real and what is imaginary. On the other hand, an organizing idea derives from your frame of reference, but it is not the same as your frame of reference. It is not as broad in its application. An organizing idea is related directly to a given set of information and to no other set. It is the shape a frame of reference takes when you direct that frame of reference to a particular set of information.

Evidence is the information you use to support your organizing idea. All evidence is information, but not all information is evidence. Evidence is any piece of information that helps to support, clarify, or develop the organizing idea of a statement.

Understanding the concepts of Part 1 is necessary to understanding the concepts of later chapters. If you are not certain about what they mean or what purpose they have, you may wish to consult your instructor before going on. As you proceed, focus your attention on what happens when you write. As you grow more familiar with the writing process, you can learn to recognize and use your own writing habits to the best advantage.

An Illustration of the Concepts in Part 1

Suppose the subject is scuba diving. A possible frame of reference might be: "Daring experiences are enjoyable. A responsible person takes proper precautions."

The writer has listed the following information:

1. regulators should be cleaned yearly
2. tanks should be tested regularly
3. carelessness in diving has a high price
4. check o-rings on tanks and always carry spares
5. scuba diving requires caution
6. everything must be operational before a dive
7. you can be your own worst enemy
8. diving is full of adventure, but equipment needs care

9. diving in tropical waters can be fun

10. masks must be water-tight

11. diving requires technical apparatus

The writer evolves an organizing idea with respect to this particular set of information. One tentative organizing idea might be: "Taking care of your equipment is essential to safe, enjoyable scuba diving." This organizing idea expresses the writer's frame of reference (the importance of caution) in terms of the information to be included in the statement. By relating that information in a logical pattern, the writer turns it into evidence that supports the tentative organizing idea.

The following paragraph develops a tentative organizing idea that is consistent with the frame of reference about the importance of caution. Notice that item 9 from the set above does not occur in the paragraph: it is information but not evidence.

Taking care of your equipment is essential to safe diving. The careless diver will discover all too soon the dangers he can encounter beneath the surface—not dangers in the water but dangers he has brought along with him. Unsafe tanks, improperly sealed masks, and clogged or damaged regulators can be the diver's most sinister enemies. Have your regulator checked professionally once a year and double check it whenever you dive. Have your tanks tested regularly and filled only by competent dive shops. Make sure you have spare o-rings and other auxiliary equipment before a dive. Always check out the gear you plan to take with you into the underwater world. Diving is as safe as the diver—enjoy its freedom and adventure but respect the apparatus that makes it possible.

DEVELOPED ORGANIZING IDEA

A responsible scuba diver checks all equipment before making a dive.

Remember that the developed organizing idea can be expressed as a sentence, but that it need not actually occur as a sentence in a paragraph or sequence of paragraphs. It is a logical component of organized discourse; it is not a grammatical component.

Do You Understand the Concepts of Part 1?

The following questions will aid you in summarizing what you have reviewed in this chapter. Try to answer them from memory.

What does a subject do?

What does an organizing idea do?

What is the difference between a frame of reference and an organizing idea?

Now Make Use of the Concepts of Part 1 in Your Own Writing

Working through the following writing situations will demonstrate your mastery of these chapters. Your instructor may suggest other situations or may encourage you to create your own.

Given any subject, you should be able to describe a frame of reference, discover an organizing idea, and select a set of evidence. You should also be able to write a statement that reflects your frame of reference and expresses your organizing idea.

Select at least three of the following subjects (or choose your own, if you prefer) and complete all steps for each.

1. the value of team sports
2. energy on a shrinking planet
3. the changing character of campus life
4. the rights of women in professional life
5. beating the system
6. the black American
7. survival in the wilderness
8. privacy in the computer age

Subject:

Frame of Reference:

Name _____ Instructor _____

Organizing Idea:

Set of Information (list at least eight items):

1.

2.

3.

4.

5.

6.

7.

8.

9.

10.

Write a paragraph that includes at least four items as evidence.

Name _____ Instructor _____

Developed Organizing Idea:

Subject:

Frame of Reference:

Organizing Idea:

Set of Information (list at least eight items):

1.

2.

3.

4.

5.

6.

7.

8.

9.

10.

Name —————————————————— Instructor ——————————————————

Write a paragraph that includes at least four items as evidence.

Developed Organizing Idea:

Subject:

Frame of Reference:

Organizing Idea:

Name ——————————————— Instructor———————————————

Set of Information (list at least eight items):

1.

2.

3.

4.

5.

6.

7.

8.

9.

10.

Write a paragraph that includes at least four items as evidence.

Name _____ Instructor _____

Developed Organizing Idea:

Part 2: Writing to Readers

7. The Reader's Frame of Reference

The chapters in Part I discussed how you assert relationships, develop an organizing idea, and find evidence to support it. Now consider your relationship to your reader. You learn about your subject by writing about it; you continue to learn about your subject through the effort to communicate your organizing idea to an intended reader.

What Role Does the Reader Play in Your Writing?

Any time you write, you have some assertions to communicate to a reader. Your communicating depends on your recognizing that there is a difference between your reader's frame of reference and your own. Communicating also depends on your recognizing that different readers have different frames of reference. Consider the following situations:

How would you describe an iceberg to a desert tribesman? Would you compare it to a snow-covered mountain, or would you compare it to a large sand dune?

Suppose you wanted to build a new supermarket. Would you tell a consumer that a new supermarket is desirable because of its long-term guarantee of profit, or would you speak instead of the convenience of neighborhood shopping? Would you tell a city councilor the same things you might tell the consumer?

Would you describe the value of the space program to a politician in terms of the theory of space flight, or would you describe it in terms of practical advantages, such as weather forecasts, improved communications, and national defense?

Would you tell fifth graders that both organic and inorganic chemistry are needed in a premed curriculum, or would you tell them that they should study science if they want to be doctors?

The Writer's Contract with the Reader

Communication in writing entails telling your intended readers what you want them to know in the way you want them to know it. In order to communicate you must consider your reader's frame of reference as you write. In any writing situation, there is a contract between the writer and the reader or readers. This contract may be stated or it may be implied. You promise to tell your reader the significance of your information, hoping that he or she will continue to read. Your reader will continue to read as long as you recognize his or her perspective. If you fail to recognize your reader's perspective, you break the contract, and the reader may stop reading. Whenever you forget the frame of reference of your reader, you fail to communicate.

You may not have thought about the reader's difficulty in understanding what you write. Since you are concerned with making assertions about your subject, you may have overlooked your reader entirely. Why bother with the reader's frame of reference? Why not just present the information and let the reader attempt to discover what is significant about it? If you know what you mean, why should your reader be puzzled?

These are common questions. They arise from a false assumption that satisfying yourself also satisfies your reader. These questions presume that your choices do not affect your reader's ability to comprehend, or that a reader can understand anything you say, any way you say it. Writers who make these assumptions feel free to write only approximately what they think they mean, believing that their readers will make the effort to understand it. But they are wrong. No such superhuman reader exists. No reader will make an effort to understand if the writer has not first made an effort to communicate.

Common experience tells you as much. Readers are only human. They are not omniscient, and they are not always completely flexible in their attitudes or their assumptions. They do not know precisely the same information the writer knows, nor do they see the world in precisely the same way. The writer cannot expect them to. The writer and the reader do not share the same asumptions about their environment, and so they do not respond to it in the same way. Their frames of reference are different.

Every time you write, you begin from a position that is different from your reader's position. Suppose you are carrying a table with two friends. They are facing you and walking backwards, and you are giving directions. Suppose you want them to turn their end of the table to your right. What would you tell them? Their frame of reference is opposite yours, and their frame of reference is the one that counts. In order to move the table to your right, you must tell them to move the table to their left.

As this example indicates, how well you communicate depends on your recognizing that your perspective differs from the perspective of any of your readers, and that their perspectives differ from each other. You have a frame of reference, but so does your reader: you see one organizing idea in a set of information, but your reader is likely to see another. You will make sense to your reader only insofar as you are able to reconcile these differences as you write.

The Effect of Your Reader's Frame of Reference

A comparison of two statements with essentially the same organizing idea, but written to two different readers, will show the difference between two frames of reference and also how that difference affects the writer's choices. Consider the following statements. Notice the selection and organization of information in each statement. See if you can recognize the kind of reader to whom each statement might have been written. Here is a list of possible readers to guide you in reader recognition.

a. a person who feels that auto races are too dangerous to be called a sport

b. a person who prefers tennis and rarely watches auto races

c. a member of the Indiana State Racing Commission

STATEMENT 1

As a racing enthusiast, I have always accepted the inevitable hazards of the sport. When cars travel at speeds approaching 200 miles per hour, serious accidents will sometimes occur. Drivers are aware of the risk in their profession and are generally willing to accept it, assuming reasonable safety measures. But the large number of fatal accidents in recent years has focused some bad publicity on the sport and made reform an issue of serious importance. Indy in particular is an old track no longer suited to the speeds of modern vehicles. I urge you, therefore, to consider design changes in both the track and the cars, thereby insuring that the tragedies of earlier seasons are not repeated in the future.

STATEMENT 2

I agree that fatal accidents in recent years have focused some bad publicity on the sport of auto racing. To prevent such serious incidents in the future, reform is essential, particularly at Indy, which is an old track unsuited to the speeds of modern vehicles. But the inevitable hazards of the sport need not overshadow its entertainment value as long as reasonable safety measures are enforced. Drivers accept the risk involved in traveling at speeds approaching 200 miles per hour and are good enough at their profession to minimize that risk. Design alterations, both in the track at Indy and in the cars that race there, are soon to be implemented. When they are, the excitement of auto racing will be matched by the quality of its safety standards.

To which of the three readers might the first statement have been written? To which might the second have been written? Both statements express essentially the same organizing idea: the writer, who is in favor of auto racing and who is concerned about its future, argues for its preservation, at the same time insisting on the need for certain reforms.

Consider how the two statements differ. Notice the beginning of each statement. In statement 1 the writer opens by declaring enthusiasm for auto racing. In statement 2 the writer opens by admitting the hazards of the sport. What do these beginnings indicate about the intended readers?

Each of these writers makes strategic choices by anticipating the reader's perspective. It is reasonable to assume that a member of the racing commission might recognize the need for reform but still might eagerly support racing as a sport. If you wish to communicate your view of racing to this reader, would you begin by insisting on its high mortality rate? Such an opening would invite immediate argument and might alienate the reader from the start. A more effective opening would be to express your enjoyment of racing first and then secondarily to assert the need for reform.

Would you make the same assumptions about a reader opposed to auto racing that you would make about the racing commissioner? Obviously not. It is more likely that the opponent of racing would fear the hazards of the sport. It is also likely that this opponent would need a lot of convincing about its entertainment value. How well would you communicate to this reader if you began by asserting your own enthusiasm for the sport? An opening that asserts enthusiasm would alienate this reader because it would ignore the reader's immediate concerns. A better opening might be to admit the hazards and the need for reform. Later on you could argue for the enjoyment of the sport if safety were insured.

Statement 1, therefore, is probably aimed at reader c, the racing commissioner, while statement 2 is probably aimed at reader a, the opponent of auto racing. In each case, the reader's perspective has affected the writer's strategy for presenting information. In statement 1 the writer begins with an expression of enthusiasm for auto racing, thereby anticipating the reader's frame of reference. Only after acknowledging the similar perspectives between reader and writer does the writer assert the necessity of reform.

In statement 2 the strategy is the same. The writer recognizes the intended reader's argument, namely, racing's high death rate, right at the beginning. The writer then concedes the need for reform. Only later, having already anticipated the reader's major objections, does the writer argue for the value of the sport. Each statement acknowledges the reader's frame of reference as it conveys the writer's organizing idea.

This strategy can result in other choices for developing paragraphs, but whatever choices you make, your concern for your reader's frame of reference influences your selection of information. By using your reader's frame of reference, you can judge the most effective way to communicate your assertions.

What Does It Mean to Focus on a Reader?

Communication requires that you present and develop your organizing idea in a way that accommodates your reader's frame of reference as well as your own. You must anticipate what your reader is capable of understanding or acknowledging. Your task is to state the significance of your information in such a way that your reader can comprehend the assertions you are making. To accomplish this task you must acknowledge your reader's frame of reference. In other words, you must focus on the reader.

To focus on a reader is to anticipate that reader's response. You do this by guessing what feelings, assumptions, experiences, or values will determine that reader's response to any subject. It does not mean that you must compromise your organizing idea merely because the reader might not agree with it. It does mean that you make use of the reader's persective in order to get started with the development of your organizing idea.

You acknowledge your reader's perspective by trying to anticipate what question the reader will raise about your organizing idea. The act of reading always implies a basic question in the reader's mind about the significance of your organizing idea to his or her frame of reference. "What does it mean to me?" the reader asks. This implied question is the reader's attempt to judge your organizing idea in terms of his or her feelings, assumptions, experiences, or values. The more you anticipate this implied question, the better your statement will acknowledge the reader's frame of reference.

You can develop the same organizing idea for two or more readers. In each case you anticipate the same question: "What does it mean to me?" In each case, however, the answer will cause you to present your organizing idea somewhat differently: you will probably begin differently and select differently from your set of information to accomplish the same end. Readers can learn something new only if they are able to relate it to what they already know. You can develop your organizing idea, therefore, precisely in terms of the reader's implied question.

In Chapters 8 and 9 you will see how to choose and organize information in a way that accommodates a given reader's frame of reference. But first, in this chapter, you will see some examples of how writing can focus on readers, so that you will recognize the differences among readers and the consequences of those differences.

An Illustration of Focusing on Different Readers

In each of the sentences below the writer states a similar idea, namely, that it takes a long time to become a medical doctor. What the writer changes is the choice of information, depending on the intended reader. See if you can tell the most probable reader to whom each sentence might have been written. Use the following list to help you with your selection.

LIST OF POSSIBLE READERS

a. a college freshman considering a premed major

b. a practicing physician

c. a fifth grader who wants someday to become a doctor

d. the parents of a college freshman considering a premed major

STATEMENTS

1. Becoming a doctor is time-consuming and expensive; both students and their families must be equally committed if the prospective M.D. is to survive the demanding years that lie ahead.

2. It takes a long time to become a doctor; only very bright people who have spent many years in school are allowed to practice medicine.

3. According to the premed curriculum, an individual must complete at least eight undergraduate courses in biology and chemistry before beginning an advanced program at an accredited medical school qualified to grant the M.D. degree.

The most probable reader to whom statement 1 was written is reader d: the parents. Can you see why?

STATEMENT 1
Becoming a doctor is time-consuming and expensive; both students and their families must be equally committed if the prospective M.D. is to survive the demanding years that lie ahead.

Would time and expense be relevant to a fifth grader? Would a doctor need to be told that medical school is a long and costly endeavor?
This sentence emphasizes that the parents and family must be prepared to share in the demands of a medical school commitment,

particularly the financial burden. Statement 1, therefore, accommodates the perspective of the student's parents by focusing on what they need to know.

The most probable reader to whom statement 2 was written is reader c: the fifth grader. Can you see why?

STATEMENT 2

It takes a long time to become a doctor; only very bright people who have spent many years in school are allowed to practice medicine.

This sentence generalizes. It includes only information that a young child could understand. It is careful not to include more complex facts about the exact length of schooling, the academic programs, the finances, and other matters with which the child would be totally unfamiliar.

The most probable reader to whom statement 3 was written is reader a: the college freshman. Can you see why?

STATEMENT 3

According to the premed curriculum, an individual must complete at least eight undergraduate courses in biology and chemistry before beginning an advanced program at an accredited medical school qualified to grant the M.D. degree.

This sentence provides detailed information rather than generalizations about the program of study needed for the M.D. It provides only the particular facts the student would need in order to make a decision about medical school. Neither a grade school student nor a parent would ordinarily need such concrete information.

Summary

You learn about your subject by explaining the significance of your information to your intended reader. You explain this significance first by acknowledging the reader's frame of reference: the feelings, assumptions, experiences, or values that cause that reader to ask, "What does it mean to me?" Anticipating this question will help you to develop your own organizing idea.

Name _____ Instructor _____

Do You Understand the Concept of Addressing Different Readers?

The following questions will aid you in summarizing what you have learned in this chapter.

What must a writer do to communicate to any reader?

A reader always has a certain amount of difficulty understanding what a writer is trying to say. Why is this so?

Explain what it means to focus on a reader.

What is the reader's implied question?

Now See If You Can Recognize Communications to Different Readers

Working through the following writing situations will demonstrate your mastery of this chapter. Your instructor may suggest other situations or may encourage you to create your own.

You should be able to recognize the most appropriate reader toward whom a particular statement might be directed; that is, you should be able to recognize the relationship between a given statement and the reader for whom it was probably written.

Listed below are two sets of sentences and one set of paragraphs. Notice that each set reflects a single basic organizing idea, expressed in different ways in each sentence or paragraph of the set. The difference in the expression of that organizing idea is due to the writer's acknowledgment of the frame of reference of a given reader. Your task is to identify the most probable reader for whom each sentence and paragraph is intended. For each set:

1. Select a reader for whom each sentence or paragraph in the set is probably intended.
2. Explain your choices in detail.

SET 1

The writer's tentative organizing idea is that the advantages of building a new supermarket complex outweigh the disadvantages.

Set of Possible Readers:

a. rival supermarket executive
b. a consumer who lives in the vicinity of the store

c. the writer's employer, president of the company

d. a city councilor

e. director of the local tennis club

Statements:

1. You are certainly right about the short-term financial risk involved, but we ought to weigh that against the considerable profit guaranteed if the project works out.

2. I believe you will find that the ease and convenience of neighborhood shopping will more than compensate for whatever minor physical changes the neighborhood will undergo.

3. The long-range advantages of this project for the community as a whole far outweigh any short-term inconvenience it may cause to local residents.

Most probable reader for whom statement 1 was written:

Explain your choice in detail:

Most probable reader for whom statement 2 was written:

Explain your choice in detail:

Most probable reader for whom statement 3 was written:

Explain your choice in detail:

SET 2

The writer is a United Nations official from a small European nation. The writer's tentative organizing idea is that there is a need for arms limitation agreements.

Set of Possible Readers:

a. representative from a major (nuclear) power who basically disagrees with the political philosophy of the country that this official represents

b. representative from a small (nonnuclear) country who is usually hostile to the political philosophy of the country that this official represents

c. representative from a major (nuclear) power who basically agrees with the political philosophy of the country that this official represents

Statements:

1. The major powers could exploit their lust for power to so griev-ous an extent that the world as a whole is thrown into jeopardy. Arms limitation agreements are therefore vital if the world is to survive its new potential for self-destruction.

2. Any great power can translate its disagreement with another power, whatever the merits of that disagreement, into terms of worldwide holocaust. Arms limitation agreements are therefore vital if the world is to survive its new potential for self-destruction.

3. Other nations who ignore the humane principles of our two na-tions would be unrestricted in their capacity to tyrannize their neighbors. Arms limitation agreements are therefore vital if the world is to survive its new potential for self-destruction.

Most probable reader for whom statement 1 was written:

Explain your choice in detail:

Most probable reader for whom statement 2 was written:

Explain your choice in detail:

Most probable reader for whom statement 3 was written:

Explain your choice in detail:

SET 3

The writer's tentative organizing idea is that smokers must pay for the entire cost of their habit.

Set of Possible Readers:

a. an executive of a major tobacco firm who is concerned about the industry's growth

b. a smoker who feels that cigarettes are already too expensive

c. a doctor who is involved in research

d. a politician who must either support or reject a bill to raise the tobacco tax

Set of Paragraphs:

1. The increase in tobacco tax has contributed to the increase in the price of cigarettes. Many smokers feel that they are being unfairly penalized by the government's decision to raise the tax. They feel that the increase in tobacco taxes places an unfair financial burden on the smoker. Yet, there is increasing evidence that the newly raised taxes do not even now cover the hidden costs of smoking. For example, the rise in heart and lung diseases has been attributed to cigarette smoking. Medical care and research for these diseases is so prohibitively expensive that it must be shared by all taxpayers, not merely by the smokers themselves. A higher cigarette tax would place the financial burden on the smoker who continues to smoke despite his awareness of the medical risks he is taking.

2. Americans today are already unhappy about the taxes they pay. It would seem obvious that any further increase in taxes would meet with immediate opposition. The tobacco tax, however, is a special case. There is increasing evidence that the tobacco tax does not fully cover the hidden costs of smoking. For example, the government spends enormous amounts of money on research for lung cancer and other diseases related directly to smoking. The revenue earned from taxes on tobacco does not cover the costs of all this medical research. The money comes from the majority of taxpayers who are nonsmokers. The cost of this research should be paid by those taxpayers who create the need for it. The tax on tobacco should be increased.

Most probable reader for whom paragraph 1 was written:

Explain your choice in detail:

Most probable reader for whom paragraph 2 was written:

Explain your choice in detail:

8. Writing to Your Intended Reader

As you recall, Chapter 7 emphasized the concept of a reader's unique frame of reference. The chapter explained that this perspective is not only different from the writer's perspective but also different from the perspective of other readers. You were shown how the same set of information could be developed differently for different frames of reference, in answer to the reader's implied question.

In this chapter you will have the chance to build your own set of information and direct a statement to different readers based on that information. You will be able to do this by using the reader's implied question. Moreover, this chapter will explain how writing to a reader's frame of reference simplifies your development of an organizing idea.

Using Your Reader's Perspective

Suppose you are talking to a class of eighth graders about the importance of nutrition. Would you discuss in detail the hazards of chemical substitutes as you might to an undergraduate majoring in nutrition? Would you outline a balanced diet as you might to a person who is responsible for planning family meals? Probably not. You would choose information by keeping in mind an eighth grader's frame of reference. In each case, your listener or reader brings a different perspective to your subject. Communicating depends on your focusing your organizing idea on the implied question derived from any reader's perspective: "What does it mean to me?"

Consider the following situation. You are an encyclopedia salesman writing letters to two prospective customers. You have talked with each of them before. Both are parents, both are in their late forties, and both own their own houses. The first is an automobile mechanic, the second is a store clerk; the first has books all around the house, the second has only a few magazines; the first is in a higher income bracket than the second. One feels that his children must go to college; the other feels that his children probably will not attend college.

Your organizing idea is that every home needs an encyclopedia. Would you write the same letter to both of these customers? Obviously not, because their frames of reference are different. But it is easier and faster to write each letter when you consider each reader's perspective in terms of the same implied question: "Why do I need an encyclopedia?"

What can you estimate about each reader? Both might have good reasons for not buying an encyclopedia. The mechanic's argument might go this way: "With all the other books we have in the house and a library down the street, why do we need an encyclopedia?" Your task would be to anticipate this question when you select your information. Can you think of information that might help you answer this question? On the other hand, the clerk's argument might be this: "I don't have any other books around; the children do enough reading in school; so why should I bother with the expense of an encyclopedia?" If you can anticipate some version of these questions, you will be able to start each letter by accommodating each reader's perspective.

In neither case do you need to compromise your frame of reference or your organizing idea just because your reader may disagree with it. Nor should you try to manipulate the reader by pretending that your perspectives are identical. Instead, you can present the same organizing idea in a way that enables each intended reader to understand it more readily.

By acknowledging the reader's implied question, you can gain two benefits. One benefit is that you will keep the reader interested; the other benefit is that you will simplify your own task. It is easier and faster to organize for someone else than it is to organize for yourself. It is easier and faster to discover what you want to say when you let your reader's frame of reference guide you in selecting and arranging information. If you can anticipate your reader's implied question, your choices are already directed toward some kinds of information and away from others. Since you can select many things to say about any subject, you can use your reader to guide and limit your choices. If you think in terms of what your reader needs to know, you can save time and effort deciding what you want to say.

An Illustration of Writing to an Intended Reader

Assume you are writing to two different readers about the rights of women. Your two readers' frames of reference are evidently different, but your organizing idea is the same: "There should be a steady movement toward equality for women, but complete equality cannot be achieved all at once." You have selected the following information for your statements:

1. equal pay for equal work
2. men and women should enjoy equal status within families
3. militancy is dangerous and ineffectual
4. consciousness raising
5. protests and demonstrations only cause aggravation

Your first reader is a male business executive. You understand that this executive prefers peace and tranquility to social chaos, whatever the merits of the dissident cause. This preference constitutes part of his frame of reference. He reacts strongly to what he believes: that the women's rights movement is composed of noisy, disruptive women who have created more problems than they have solved. He might ask, "Where is all this commotion leading us?" Or he might ask, more specifically, "What inconvenience will the women's movement cost me?" You might consider either of these to be this reader's implied question. Or you might anticipate some other version of them.

The following statement illustrates one way to present your organizing idea to this reader. In this case, you might acknowledge the reader's frame of reference by first presenting information that the reader is already disposed to accept. Then you might argue the case by consistently acknowledging this reader's prior assumptions, but without compromising your organizing idea. Here is how such a paragraph might develop.

> The noisy and disruptive protests of the more militant women's groups have caused irritation to many people during the last few years. But this irritation should not blind us to the fact that these groups have a good deal to complain about. For example, industry has always prided itself on judging a person solely on the basis of performance, but it has traditionally paid women less and promoted them more slowly than their male counterparts. We can't have complete equality tomorrow; there must be more consciousness raising among both men and women before that occurs. But a steady movement toward male-female equality in social relations and in business must continue. Otherwise, in denying half the population the rights supposedly guaranteed to all, we justify the protests.

If you attack your reader's assumptions, your reader will probably reject your organizing idea. On the other hand, you can acknowledge your reader's assumptions and then use those assumptions to introduce what you want to say: "Granted the protests are noisy, yet they have some justification"; "granted some progress has been made, but there is much yet to be done"; "granted we cannot have instantaneous equality at the cost of drastic social upheaval, but we are obligated to guarantee to others the rights we so zealously defend for ourselves."

Now for the second reader. Suppose this reader is a law student. The reader's opinion is that equality between men and women must be constitutionally protected—at once, in all areas, at all costs. His implied question might be something like this: "How do we get started?" or "What must be done to enable these changes to occur?"

Can you approach this reader as you did the business executive? Will your decisions be the same? Here is a statement that might anticipate the frame of reference of your second reader. Notice how it differs from the first statement in the way it acknowledges some assumptions about "the need for equality."

> The subordinate place of women in the past justifies the current drive for equal rights. But overmilitancy, which creates resentment rather than understanding, does not aid this campaign. Five thousand years of social history cannot be changed in a single

generation. Men and women will receive equal pay before they have equal family responsibilities. Any attempt to legislate immediate equality in all fields will lead to resentment among men and women. Accordingly, they will avoid compliance. The answer to sexual equality is education, the raising of men's social consciousness as well as of women's. Education rather than demonstrations is the key to equality.

What to Do If You Cannot Identify Your Reader

Writing to an unknown reader is a situation that news and magazine writers, for example, confront every day. These writers direct their statements not to an individual person but to a set of traits that characterize their readers' frames of reference. In other words, these writers focus on traits that their readers have in common. Every newspaper and magazine assumes a typical reader and focuses on the traits of that reader. The intended reader of *Argosy* is obviously different from the intended reader of *Cosmopolitan.* The intended reader of *Time* is different from the intended reader of *U.S. News and World Report.* One can readily estimate a reader's approximate age, knowledge of a given subject, political affiliation, social class, annual income, moral values, personal interests, and many other things as well. Writers for these publications select and organize their information keeping in mind the characteristics that their readers share, although the writers do not know the individuals who are going to buy the newspaper or magazine.

Whenever your are uncertain of the individual who might be your reader, you can take advantage of a construct called the Common Reader, just as journalists do. Writing to this Common Reader is often preferable to addressing an individual because the Common Reader's frame of reference is more easily recognizable than that of any individual. Although you might often be mistaken or unsure about the unique and continually changing frame of reference of a given individual, the characteristics of a Common Reader are constant, and they apply to everyone. If you focus on these characteristics, you will find that the Common Reader can be your most reliable guide in many writing situations.

The Characteristics of the Common Reader

The Common Reader is a model that you construct in your mind, an all-purpose reader that you create on the basis of characteristics that all readers share. In order to use the Common Reader you must first recognize these characteristics.

There are two characteristics that all readers share, and these are the major traits of the Common Reader. The most important is the reader's **ignorance of your organizing idea.** The Common Reader may know a great deal about your subject in general, but the Common Reader does not know your organizing idea. In other words, no reader knows your organizing idea before you convey it. Remember that no reader is omniscient. Any reader needs all the guidance you can give about how you are developing your organizing idea.

The second major characteristic of the Common Reader is **impatience.** The Common Reader wants you to get to the point. Any reader wants to know the significance of your assertions. Whatever you are going to say will modify the reader's understanding of your subject, and naturally the reader is impatient to find out the significance of your organizing idea.

The Common Reader, then, is a construct that you build in your mind, based on what is true of all readers, namely, their ignorance of your organizing idea and their impatience. These two traits are what make the concept of the Common Reader so reliable. You can use them no matter whom you address.

In addition to these two major traits of the Common Reader, there are three others that are less important but useful. If you wish, you can individualize the Common Reader by making three assumptions that will work most of the time. Assume three ways in which the Common Reader is like you. The Common Reader has reached the **same level of maturity** that you have reached, has achieved about the **same level of formal education** that you have achieved, and knows **approximately as much as you do about your subject.** This last similarity should not mislead you. Knowing about your subject is not the same as knowing your organizing idea.

You might ask, "Why these three characteristics and not others?" The answer is that addressing these characteristics will help you sound more like yourself. You are already familiar with frames of reference that are typical of your own level of maturity, your own level of education, and your own knowledge of the subject. If you focus on these three minor traits in the Common Reader, your writing will sound more natural. To summarize: with these two major traits and three lesser traits you can reasonably assume that the Common Reader has a frame of reference that is very similar to your own. The Common Reader is interested in what you are trying to say but impatient to know your organizing idea.

There is a crucial distinction here. The distinction is between writing merely to yourself, which denies communication, and writing to someone else, which enables communication. You want to write to someone else because your purpose is to communicate. The construct of the Common Reader is a convenient way for you to acknowledge your reader. The Common Reader keeps you from writing to yourself, but in a way that feels natural. If you happen to have specific information about your reader, then use it; if not, then the frame of reference represented by your Common Reader will be a useful guide in whatever you write.

Summary

You focus on a reader to keep that reader interested and to simplify the task of writing. Acknowledging the reader's frame of reference gains you a better hearing for your organizing idea. It also gives you the means of presenting it without compromise. Acknowledging the reader's perspective serves you equally well with a known reader or the Common Reader.

Do You Understand the Concept of Writing to an Intended Reader?

The following questions will aid you in summarizing what you have learned in this chapter.

What are the two benefits you gain by focusing your organizing idea on your reader's frame of reference?

What kinds of information would you select to tell an eighth grader about the value of nutrition? Write down four or five pieces of information in the space below (use complete sentences).

What kinds of information would you select to tell a family meal planner about the value of nutrition? Write down four or five pieces of information in the space below.

What kinds of information would you select to tell the local weight watchers club about the value of nutrition? Write down four or five pieces of information in the space below.

What characteristics of the Common Reader are shared by all readers?

Now Make Use of the Concept of Writing to an Intended Reader

Working through the following writing situations will demonstrate your mastery of this chapter. Your instructor may suggest other situations or encourage you to create your own.

You should be able to convey any organizing idea to different readers by acknowledging each reader's frame of reference.

Here are two different writing situations. You are the writer. For each situation:

1. Describe your own frame of reference.

2. List a set of information related to the subject.

3. State an organizing idea.

4. Select a reader, describe this reader's frame of reference, and suggest the reader's implied question.

5. Write a paragraph to this reader.

6. Select a second reader and describe this reader's frame of reference.

7. Write a paragraph to this second reader.

SUBJECT 1
the advantages of an encyclopedia in every home

Your Frame of Reference:

Your Set of Information:

1.

2.

3.

4.

5.

Your Organizing Idea:

Your Readers:
1. the automobile mechanic described earlier in this chapter
2. the store clerk described earlier in this chapter
3. a fourteen-year-old who might persuade his or her parents to buy an encyclopedia
4. a free-lance photographer, unmarried, living in an apartment

Name _____ Instructor _____

Possible frame of reference of Reader 1 (list traits and suggest the reader's implied question):

Paragraph(s) to Reader 1 (remember that each paragraph must have an organizing idea):

Paragraph(s) to Reader 1 (continued):

Name _____ Instructor_____

Paragraph(s) to Reader 1 (continued):

Possible Frame of Reference of Reader 2 (list traits and suggest the reader's implied question):

Paragraph(s) to Reader 2 (remember that each paragraph must have an organizing idea):

Name _____ Instructor_____

Paragraph(s) to Reader 2 (continued):

Paragraph(s) to Reader 2 (continued):

WRITING TO READERS

SUBJECT 2

conformity versus nonconformity: accepting "the system" or opposing it

Your Frame of Reference:

Your Set of Information:

1.

2.

3.

4.

5.

Your Organizing Idea:

Your Readers:

1. a former campus radical of the 1960s
2. a psychiatrist who has defined mental health in terms of conforming to social and cultural norms
3. a priest who has recently written an article attacking the idea of marriage in the priesthood
4. a person who has served three years in prison for draft evasion
5. a black mayor of any large city in the United States

Possible Frame of Reference of Reader 1 (list traits and suggest the reader's implied question):

Name _____ Instructor_____

Paragraph(s) to Reader 1 (remember that each paragraph must have an organizing idea):

Paragraph(s) to Reader 1 (continued):

Possible Frame of Reference of Reader 2 (list traits and suggest the reader's implied question):

Paragraph(s) to Reader 2 (remember that each paragraph must have an organizing idea):

Paragraph(s) to Reader 2 (continued):

Name _____ Instructor _____

Paragraph(s) to Reader 2 (continued):

9. Evidence for the Reader

You recall that evidence was defined in Chapter 5 as any piece of information that clarifies and supports your organizing idea. There is another factor to consider in selecting evidence. The information must not only support your organizing idea, but it must also accommodate your reader's frame of reference. The way to choose evidence by accommodating that other frame of reference is the subject of this chapter.

The Best Evidence Is Functional Evidence

You can determine the best evidence to use in a given writing situation by considering the kinds of information your intended reader needs to know in order to understand your organizing idea. You have seen in Chapters 7 and 8 that focusing on your reader helps you to discover and organize what you want to say. Although you do not change your organizing idea in addressing different readers, you often change or rearrange the evidence you use. The reader you have in mind directly affects the choices you make about what to include and what to omit.

The definition of evidence in Chapter 5 can now be expanded to include what you know about readers. The best evidence is that set of information that most clearly and effectively conveys your organizing idea to your intended reader. The best evidence is functional evidence.

Some pieces of information are more useful as evidence because they support your organizing idea in terms of your reader's frame of reference. Other pieces of information may not be useful to you, even though they could be related to what you want to say, because they do not focus on your reader's perspective. They would not be useful, for example, if they were too obvious, given the reader's knowledge of the subject, or if they were too confusing, given the reader's frame of reference.

Consider the following set of information related to the subject, "language." Which items do you think an average eighth grader would understand? Put a check opposite those items as you read.

1. The term "morpheme" has become almost meaningless as a label of speech components.
2. Phonetic transcriptions of speech tend to differ from one transcriber to the next and are not always reliable guides to the speech-act.
3. Language is often described in terms of sounds, words, and word combinations.
4. The "parts of speech" are derived from Latin grammar and are not especially helpful in describing English syntax.
5. The parts of speech are: noun, pronoun, verb, adverb, adjective, conjunction, preposition, and interjection.
6. Acoustical phonetics is generally supposed to provide more reliable and detailed information about speech than articulatory phonetics.
7. People who study the components of speech are called linguists.

Suppose you were writing about "the constituents of speech." Suppose you were writing one statement to students in junior high school and another statement to college students specializing in linguistics. All of the items in the list could be related to your subject or to an organizing idea concerning "the constituents of speech." But are all of them useful as evidence if your reader is an eighth grader? (How many did you check?) Look at the list again. Do your choices remain the same if you are writing to a group of college linguistics majors?

Items 1, about the morpheme, 2, about phonetic transcriptions, and 6, about acoustical phonetics, might be of interest to college students but would be too complex for most younger students.

Item 3, which describes the speech-act in a general way, would be useful for the younger student, but it would actually be false information in a statement to a student of linguistics (since "word" is not defined in the same way by linguists).

Item 7, which defines linguistics, might be appropriate information for a young student, but it would be superfluous to a linguistics major.

Every item in this list requires the same kind of decision. Choices about functional evidence in these two writing situations result from the recognition that the perspectives of these two intended readers are different. In any writing situation the information you choose as evidence for your statement must be evaluated both in terms of its relevance to your organizing idea and its relevance to your reader's frame of reference. These two criteria, taken together, define functional evidence.

An Illustration of Finding Functional Evidence

Suppose a friend of yours is seeking an appointment to the Peace Corps. He or she is willing to undergo intensive training and receive low pay in return for working with persons in rural areas of some underdeveloped country. This friend has asked you to write a letter of recommendation. (Think of a real person; do not invent one.) You have agreed to support your friend.

Who is going to read this letter? If your answer is "the Peace Corps," you are wrong. The Peace Corps is an institution, not a reader. Similarly, you cannot write effectively to a corporation, or a bank, or a university, or a church, or a hotel: they are not readers either. Readers are people who are going to be affected by what you write and who are going to judge from their own frames of reference how effectively you have told them what you want to say. A bank does not act on your request for a loan, but a reader of loan applications does. A corporation does not consider your request for a raise, but a department head does.

The person who is going to read your letter is a reader of applications to the Peace Corps. Your knowing this reader's job helps you to determine his or her perspective. You can assume that the reader knows what to look for in a Peace Corps candidate. The reader already knows what personality traits are more desirable, or less desirable, in Peace Corps volunteers, what kinds of training and job skills are helpful, and where they can most usefully be applied. At the same time, the reader is a person who must read hundreds of letters of recommendation from writers like you about individuals like your friend. She or he must make decisions in terms of what you communicate.

Given this reader's perspective, your job is to select functional evidence for a letter of recommendation to the Peace Corps. What kinds of information would you select? Your purpose is to focus your reader's attention in such a way as to distinguish your friend from all other applicants.

1.

2.

3.

4.

5.

6.

7.

8.

(Complete this set of information before going on.) Now assess the information you have written down.

1. Does any piece of information say how long you have known your friend, or how well, or under what circumstances: school, work, neighborhood, military service, church, or bowling league?

Yes _____ No _____

This information could be helpful to a Peace Corps reader. It would reveal how well you know your friend and therefore how valid your information is likely to be. If you know your friend very well, this information would also serve as proof of the validity of your details.

2. Are there any pieces of information that describe what the Peace Corps is about or the nature of its work?

Yes _____ No _____

Your reader probably knows more about the Peace Corps than you do, so this information is useless.

3. Does any piece of information include your personal assessment of your friend's ability to do Peace Corps work?

Yes _____ No _____

This information is practically useless. It is up to the reader to decide whether your friend can do Peace Corps work. It is presumptuous of you to make this decision when you do not know the criteria this reader uses.

4. Does any piece of information include your personal assessment of the country in which your friend could be placed effectively or what kind of job would be most suitable?

Yes _____ No _____

This information is equally presumptuous. The Peace Corps reader will decide about such matters. It is your responsibility simply to give information that will help the reader to evaluate your friend.

5. Are there any pieces of information related to your friend's personality traits?

Yes _____ No _____

This information might be helpful, depending on how you present it. (See 6, 7, and 8.)

6. If you have listed personality traits, how many of them are exemplified or detailed, rather than merely labeled: "good," "kind," "enterprising," "hardworking," "reliable," "likes children and pets"? Detail is essential. Abstract virtue is no more useful than abstract people, and abstractions do not accomplish Peace Corps work. If you describe your friend merely as "generous," "benevolent," or "humanitarian," you are misleading, not helping, your reader. This reader has hundreds of recommendations to look at; if all of them catalogue abstractions, how can one applicant be distinguished from another?

7. If you have listed personality traits, how many of them are described in terms of your knowledge of your friend?
   This information reinforces your statement of how long and how well you have known your friend (see 1 above). You must demonstrate firsthand knowledge of your friend's personality and behavior; otherwise, your reader will have little confidence in what you say.

8. Are there any pieces of information related to your friend's job skills, or education, or language abilities, or special training, or experience?

   Yes _____ No _____

   This information is obviously useful, depending on how you present it and how detailed you make it.

9. If you have listed special skills, how many of them are exemplified or detailed in terms of your knowledge of your friend. What foreign language does your friend speak? Where was the training? What job experience did your friend have and for how long? Again, detail is essential. The more specific your description of your friend, the more reliable it becomes for the reader of your statement.

With this evaluation of your original information in mind, write several paragraphs to the Peace Corps reader, using your information to recommend your friend. Remember to turn that information into functional evidence for your organizing idea. You can do this by focusing on your reader as well as by developing your own organizing idea, according to the concepts you have previously learned.

YOUR TENTATIVE ORGANIZING IDEA

PARAGRAPH(S)

Summary

Focusing on your reader keeps the reader interested and simplifies the task of writing. Recognizing your reader's frame of reference helps you to select evidence for communicating with that reader. The best evidence for any statement clarifies and supports your organizing idea and accommodates your reader's frame of reference.

Do You Understand the Concept of Functional Evidence?

The following questions will aid you in summarizing what you have learned in this chapter:

What is functional evidence?

Here is another way of asking the same question. What are the two criteria for determining functional evidence?

Now Put the Concept of Functional Evidence to Work in Your Own Writing

Working through the following writing situations will demonstrate your mastery of this chapter. Your instructor may suggest other situations or encourage you to create your own.

You should be able to choose evidence for any given statement on the basis of its relevance to your organizing idea and its relevance to your reader's frame of reference.

Here are two practical writing situations that may someday apply to you. For each of these situations:

1. Identify and describe in a short paragraph the frame of reference of some intended reader.
2. Derive seven or eight pieces of information for a statement to that reader.
3. Write a statement to that reader that incorporates your information.
4. Remember to turn your information into functional evidence as you write.

WRITING SITUATION 1

a letter of application for a job to the Ford Motor Company

Intended Reader's Frame of Reference (list traits that reveal the reader's implied question):

Name _____ Instructor_____

Tentative Organizing Idea:

Set of Information:

1.

2.

3.

4.

5.

6.

7.

8.

Your letter (remember to focus on your reader while you develop your organizing idea and remember also that each paragraph must have an organizing idea):

Name _____ Instructor _____

WRITING SITUATION 2

    a letter of application for admission to any education institution.

Intended Reader's Frame of Reference (list traits that reveal the reader's implied question):

Tentative Organizing Idea:

Name _____ Instructor_____

Set of Information:

1.

2.

3.

4.

5.

6.

7.

8.

Your letter (remember to focus on your reader while you develop your organizing idea and remember also that each paragraph must have an organizing idea):

10. Review of Part 2

This chapter will serve as a review of the concepts you worked with in Part 2: focusing on an intended reader or the Common Reader, anticipating your reader's implied question, and presenting functional evidence. You should now be familiar with these concepts, and you should be able to use them when you write.

Remember Three Essential Concepts in Part 2

Focusing on an intended reader is acknowledging your reader's frame of reference. How well you communicate depends on your recognizing that your perspective differs from the perspective of any one of your readers, and that their perspectives differ from each other. You will communicate effectively to any reader to the degree that you can reconcile these differences as you write.

Writing to a reader entails using the reader's implied question as a guide to presenting and developing your organizing idea. Readers can learn something new only if they are able to relate it to what they already know. Your task, therefore, is to develop the significance of your information in such a way that your reader will be able to recognize a new pattern of relationships.

There are two reasons for focusing on an intended reader. The first reason is to keep the reader reading. If you do not anticipate your intended reader's perspective, you will lose that reader. The second reason is to simplify the task of writing. It is easier and faster to discover what you want to say when you let your reader's perspective guide you in selecting and organizing your information. The reader naturally benefits from such consideration. But you also benefit from using the reader's implied question in discovering the significance of what you are trying to say.

The Common Reader is an all-purpose reader that you create on the basis of characteristics that most readers share. You can use the Common Reader when you are not writing to a known reader. The set of characteristics that the Common Reader represents is often more reliable than those of a known reader.

The most important characteristic of the Common Reader is that reader's ignorance of your organizing idea. The Common Reader does not know your organizing idea until you have conveyed it. A second important characteristic is the Common Reader's impatience. This reader wants to know your organizing idea as soon as you discover it.

The Common Reader also has three minor characteristics: the Common Reader has achieved about the same level of maturity you have achieved, has reached your level of formal education, and knows as much as you do about your subject—but not about your organizing idea.

The Common Reader is a convenient construct. It forces you to recognize a frame of reference similar to yours but different from yours. Heeding the demands of the Common Reader prevents you from writing to yourself, which denies communication, and orients you to another perspective, which enables communication.

Functional evidence is that evidence which most clearly and persuasively conveys your organizing idea to some intended reader. To find functional evidence you decide on a set of information that most effectively communicates your organizing idea in terms of your reader's frame of reference. Functional evidence supports or clarifies your organizing idea in a way that enables a reader to comprehend it.

Understanding the concepts of Part 2 is necessary to understanding the concepts of later chapters. If you are not certain about what they mean or what purpose they have, you may wish to consult your instructor before going on. As you proceed, focus your attention on what happens when you write. As you grow more familiar with the writing process, you can learn to recognize and use your own natural writing habits to the best advantage.

An Illustration of Some Important Concepts in Part 2

Consider the following writing situation. You are an instructor in the English department at National University. You have just learned that your department is being forced to cut back its staff because of budget reductions. You must find a new teaching position for the fall.

Looking through the job listings that are published each year for the benefit of teachers seeking employment, you have noticed that World University is advertising an opening for someone who can teach nineteenth-century fiction and also freshman composition. Since these are precisely your areas of specialization, you have decided to write a letter to the chairman of the department at World U., inquiring about the opening.

Your task is to write a letter applying for this position. You must estimate what your reader, the chairman of the department, needs to know in order to evaluate your credentials and suitability. You must then select functional evidence to support your request for a position. Here are some characteristics of your intended reader.

NOTE: The format following is used simply to illustrate how the traits of any intended reader can help the writer to choose and organize information. You need not follow this format when you work through a similar problem in this chapter: simply describe the frame of reference of your intended reader in a paragraph.

INFORMATION ABOUT THE DEPARTMENT CHAIRMAN	WHAT THE INFORMATION TELLS YOU AS A WRITER
1. She is a well-known scholar who has taught for many years and has published widely.	Therefore, she has a clear understanding of academic excellence and will not be taken in by vague and self-flattering assertions about your credentials.

2. She has served as department chairman for several years and has also worked in other administrative posts within the university.

Therefore, she knows what the department's needs are and what credentials a prospective employee must have to fill those needs. She will not be impressed by generalities but will need detailed information about your field of study, your teaching experience, and your publications and scholarly work in progress.

3. She will be reading more than 600 applications for the teaching appointment World U. has advertised.

Therefore, she will not be patient with applicants whose letters are long, rambling, and overstated; she will want precise details that distinguish you from other applicants.

You have already selected the following set of information, later to become functional evidence as you develop your organizing idea:

1. I am a specialist in nineteenth-century fiction and in English composition.

2. I have taught courses in fiction, in English literature since 1800, and in writing.

3. I have been an instructor at National U. for the past two years.

4. I have directed the department's writing program.

5. My dissertation concerned the influence of nineteenth-century rhetorical theory on the major English novelists of the period.

6. I have not yet published anything, but I have written an article, based on the dissertation, called "Rhetoric and the Nineteenth-Century Literary Imagination."

7. I have directed undergraduate projects in Jane Austen and Thomas Hardy.

8. I am available for an interview at the national teachers' convention in Baltimore next month.

9. My appointment has not been renewed.

ORGANIZING IDEA

I would like you to consider my credentials for a teaching appointment at World U.

STATEMENT TO THE DEPARTMENT CHAIRMAN

(The numbers in parentheses refer to the pieces of information in the list above. Notice how the information is used in the statement. It is not always literally repeated from the set; instead, it is modified and adapted to suit your purpose as you discover what you want to say.)

I am currently an instructor in the English department at National University (3), teaching courses in writing and in the nineteenth-century novel (1). Because of the budget reductions the department has advised me that it will not be able to support me in the fall (9). According to a recent job listing, World University is anticipating an opening in my areas of specialization (1), and I am writing to you in the hope that my credentials for such a position might be suitable.

During the past two years (3) I have taught courses in nineteenth-century fiction, in English literature since 1800, and in critical writing (2). I have also directed undergraduate projects in Jane Austen's theory of the imagination and in pessimism in the novels of Thomas Hardy (7). In addition, I have administrative experience as director of the department's writing program (4).

My Ph.D. dissertation concerned the influence of nineteenth-century rhetorical theory on the major English novelists of the period (5). I would be prepared, therefore, to teach courses in the history of rhetoric as well as in nineteenth-century fiction (1). I have reworked some of my dissertation materials into an article titled "Rhetoric and the Nineteenth-Century Literary Imagination," which is now being reviewed for publication by the journal *Nineteenth-Century Fiction* (4). A copy of the article is available should you wish to see a sample of my scholarship. The abstract of my dissertation is, of course, also at your disposal.

If my credentials appear acceptable, may I hear from you? I will send my dossier at your request. I will also be present at the national teachers' convention in Baltimore next month should you decide that an interview can be arranged (8).

Do You Understand the Concepts of Part 2?

The following questions will aid you in summarizing what you have reviewed in this chapter. Try to answer them from memory.

What must you recognize about any reader, and how does the recognition assist you in making choices about what to say?

When do you use the Common Reader?

What two criteria must be satisfied if the information you have selected for a statement is to become functional evidence?

Now Make Use of the Concepts in Part 2 in Your Own Writing

Working through the following writing situations will demonstrate your mastery of this chapter. Your instructor may suggest other situations or may encourage you to create your own.

You should be able to select and describe an intended reader and write a statement to that reader that supports your organizing idea.

Following are three writing situations. For each one state your organizing idea and a set of information in the spaces provided. Then select your intended reader and specify that reader's characteristics in a short paragraph. For one of the three situations use the Common Reader as the focus for the statement. It is your responsibility to decide in which writing situation the Common Reader would be more helpful than some known reader.

NOTE: Be explicit. The more precise you are in describing your organizing idea and deriving your functional evidence, the more easily you can show your mastery of the objectives of Part 2. If you are writing to the Common Reader, list the Common Reader's major and minor characteristics. If you are writing to a known person, describe this reader's frame of reference in a way that indicates the reader's implied question.

WRITING SITUATION 1

You want to attend law school, medical school, graduate school, professional school, or vocational school (choose one). As part of your application you are writing a letter describing your intentions, your credentials, your interests, and other information about yourself. The school will use your statement as one indication of your qualifications for admission. Use actual details from your own background.

Intended Reader (describe the reader's frame of reference in a way that indicates the reader's implied question; if you choose the Common Reader, list the Common Reader's characteristics):

Name _____ Instructor_____

Set of Information (list at least eight pieces of information):

1.

2.

3.

4.

5.

6.

7.

8.

Tentative Organizing Idea:

Paragraph(s) (remember that each paragraph must have an organizing idea):

WRITING TO READERS

Name _____ Instructor_____

WRITING SITUATION 2

You are a free-lance writer doing a short essay on one of the following subjects: "the hazards of smoking," "the mystical experience," "life in the ghetto," "legalizing marijuana," or "games people play" (choose one). You are planning to submit the essay to a popular magazine. Apply your own frame of reference and your own understanding of the subject.

Intended Reader (describe the reader's frame of reference in a way that indicates the reader's implied question; if you choose the Common Reader, list the Common Reader's characteristics):

Name ————————————————— Instructor ————————————————

Set of Information (list at least eight pieces of information):

1.

2.

3.

4.

5.

6.

7.

8.

Tentative Organizing Idea:

Paragraph(s) (remember that each paragraph must have an organizing idea):

Name _____ Instructor _____

WRITING SITUATION 3

You are the assistant principal of a city high school. It is Monday morning, 9 A.M. You had left last Wednesday on a three-day assignment to an evaluation team in another city school. In your absence the principal has done your job in addition to his own.

You have finished taking care of late arrivals. You can now turn your attention to problems that collected during your absence. The most urgent problem seems to center around Stephen Davis, a student the principal had suspended last Friday. You have on your desk a report on the incident and a note from your secretary that Stephen's parents have already called this morning. Stephen has never been suspended before; he has told his parents that he was suspended because of an overdue library book, and they are pretty upset.

According to the report a library book was certainly part of the problem; Stephen took from the library a reference book plainly marked "for library use only." The book was needed for a report that had to be completed by all the students in his social studies class. When the book disappeared, the social studies teacher questioned several students, including Stephen, who had been in the library immediately before the theft. All denied having taken the book. The teacher was suspicious, and after obtaining permission from the principal, she had Stephen's locker opened. The book was inside. Presented with the evidence of the theft, Stephen used "threatening and obscene language" to the teacher. The incident was witnessed by three students. The teacher then sent the student to the principal who ordered a suspension. He instructed Stephen to return in three days with his parents.

Your standard procedure in cases of this kind is to find out as much as possible about the student before talking to the parents. The guidance office contributes the following information:

- Stephen is sixteen years old.

- He has two sisters; one was graduated last June, an honor student, active in class organizations.

- His father owns a contracting business in a neighboring city. He is not a college graduate.

- His mother has long been active in civic affairs and was recently named to the city planning board.

Stephen's guidance counselor, who is responsible for a large number of students, has seen him only once, and his comments are not very informative: "seems pleasant," "rather quiet."

Stephen's academic performance, you find, has been erratic. He has a "D" average in math though he was a "B" math student in junior high school. He has an "A" in science. His science teacher, whom you meet in the teachers' lounge, says that he is one of the best students in the class, and that his science project, a hydraulic pump, shows more creativity than he has seen in several years. Stephen has a "C" in social studies and a "C+" in English.

His disciplinary record shows that he has been on detention twice in the past semester, once for excessive talking in English class and once for the same offense in math class. His record does not show any previous disciplinary problems in social studies.

Finally, with all this information in mind, you talk to the social studies teacher. She has taught in the school for four years and you have heard no complaints about her performance. She can add little to the report.

You now have to inform the parents of the real situation before their conference with you and the principal. You must describe the situation, and make clear why their son was suspended. At the same time you must solicit their aid in dealing with their son's problem, and you must avoid simply redirecting their anger away from the school administration and toward their son.

With all this in mind, write a letter to Stephen Davis' parents.

Intended Reader (describe the reader's frame of reference in a way that indicates the reader's implied question; if you choose the Common Reader, list the Common Reader's characteristics):

Set of Information (list at least eight pieces of information):

1.

2.

3.

4.

5.

6.

7.

8.

Tentative Organizing Idea:

Name _____ Instructor _____

Paragraph(s) (remember that each paragraph must have an organizing idea):

Paragraph(s) (continued)

Name _____ Instructor _____

Part 3: Building an Argument

11. A Functional Sequence

Parts 1 and 2 stated that writing is a process of selecting and organizing information about a given subject in a way that will enable your reader to understand what you want to say. The chapters in Parts 1 and 2 explained how you learn about your subject by developing organizing ideas and deriving functional evidence. These chapters also explained how to communicate your organizing idea by acknowledging your reader's frame of reference.

Once you have a set of information and a tentative organizing idea, you must determine, as you write, where any given piece of information belongs; that is, you must decide how to sequence your information. In this chapter you will see how your sequence depends on the order in which your reader needs to know what you are trying to communicate.

What Is a Functional Sequence of Information?

Language conveys information in temporal sequence. Unlike the information in a snapshot or a painting, a verbal message is not revealed instantaneously. It is revealed as a linear succession of events. These events are separate but related. Segments of information, expressed in words, phrases, sentences, paragraphs, and groups of paragraphs, overlap each other in various ways. Verbal meaning evolves, therefore, through a linear series of associations. Sentence by sentence, paragraph by paragraph, your statement evolves in time, developing from one assertion to the next until you are satisfied that your statement is complete.

Because verbal structures are linear, your task as a writer is to construct a functional sequence for the information you want to present. You choose an order for your various pieces of information. You decide what should come first and what should follow, and you make this decision repeatedly as you write.

Fortunately, you can look to your intended reader for help in deciding on a sequence of information. Just as you use the reader's frame of reference in choosing functional evidence (as you saw in Chapter 9), you also use the reader's frame of reference to guide you in ordering that evidence through every paragraph of your evolving statement. A functional sequence of information is one that accommodates the reader's need to understand the significance of some information before he or she can understand the significance of information that comes later.

The Inverted-Pyramid Model of Functional Sequence

New writers, for example, allow themselves to be guided by the frames of reference of their intended readers. Specifically, they present their information in an order that satisfies the priorities of their readers. By using a sequence that accommodates the readers' priorities, they can write rapidly under the pressure of daily deadlines.

The model that news writers follow is called the inverted pyramid. It is not the only model of functional sequence. It is not even the best one (this text will describe a more comprehensive model), but its simplicity makes it a good one to start with. The inverted pyramid reconciles the writer's learning process with the reader's needs; that is, it reconciles a discrepancy between the way the writer perceives the significance of information with the way the reader perceives it. Knowing about this discrepancy is essential for your understanding of a functional sequence.

As you learned in Chapters 2 and 3, writers begin with some notion of what they want to say, but it is only approximate. Your learning process, when you write, consists of discovering the significance of your information by means of making assertions about relationships. Whatever significance you discover is largely the result of your writing.

In other words, you naturally progress from gathering information about a subject to making assertions that state the significance of that information.

Readers, on the other hand, initially need some sense of that significance in order to see how the writer connects pieces of information. Readers need to know the writer's organizing idea before they can assess or appreciate the relevance of other information in the writer's statement.

To communicate, therefore, is to invert the result of your natural learning process. You first present a tentative organizing idea about your information to accommodate the opposed priorities of the reader. You begin your statement with an assertion of the significance of what you are about to relate and a declaration of the direction in which you will explore your subject. This inversion is what news writers use. It gives them a ready means of presenting information: they begin with what the reader most needs to know, and then they provide relevant information in a decreasing order of importance.

Your reader first needs to know your organizing idea before comprehending the importance of any single piece of information. By revealing the significance of your information as soon as possible, therefore, you make your statement easier to follow. Your reader's estimate of the value of any piece of evidence will be far more accurate if you have initially stated the organizing idea that the evidence is designed to support.

The inverted-pyramid model requires an inversion of your natural movement from pieces of information to developed organizing idea. This inversion allows you to accommodate your reader's need to know your conclusion before you present supporting information. This sequence of priorities is the essence of the inverted pyramid, and it is typified by news writing.

The inverted pyramid can be diagrammed. First, assume that the writer's learning process is represented by this pyramid:

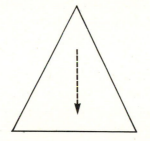

This representation signifies that the writer normally moves toward a broader conclusion (the base of the pyramid). The reader's priorities can then be represented by an inverted pyramid:

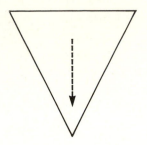

This representation shows that the reader needs to know about the conclusion before comprehending the separate pieces of information.

Inverting your own natural learning process will anticipate the needs of your intended reader. In other words, you invert Model I of the learning process to achieve Model II:

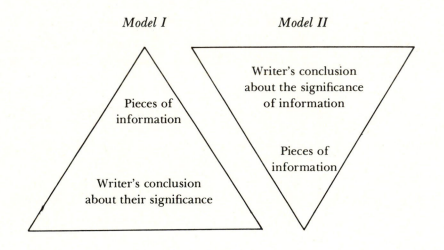

In news writing the reader's need to know the writer's most significant assertion dictates the sequence of information. The news story proceeds from the most significant assertion to the least significant assertion. As you read through a typical news story, therefore, you find that more and more is said about less and less. The typical news story can be diagrammed this way:

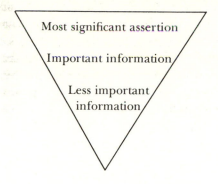

Most significant assertion

Important information

Less important
information

Consider the following set of information as an example. What would be the most significant piece of information to a newspaper reader? What information is less important?

1. it has been snowing all week in Denver
2. plane carries load of Christmas mail
3. plane develops trouble with navigational equipment
4. plane approaches landing in Denver
5. plane is observed to be off course
6. plane crashes

These events are listed as they occurred, in a chronological sequence. But the order in which the events occurred does not satisfy the reader's sense of their significance. A news story would probably begin with the fact that the plane crashed (6), since this is what the reader would need to know in order to understand the importance of the other pieces of information in the set.

Items 3, about navigational equipment, 4, about the landing approach, and 5, about the error in the plane's course, are important details, though not necessarily in that order (of course, if it were a Denver newspaper, 4 would suddenly become much more important information, given the perspective of a Denver newspaper reader). Items 1, about the weather, and 2, about Christmas mail, are less significant.

The news writer's sequence, therefore, would probably be something like this: 6; 3, 4, and 5; 1 and 2. Although the sequence is not strictly predictable, item by item, the general direction is from item 6 as the most significant assertion to item 2 as the least significant. Notice again that the newspaper sequence is not based on chronology but on the reader's sense of what is important. This perspective is the essence of the inverted pyramid.

The Inverted Pyramid in Detail

Read through the assertions given below. They are taken from an actual news story, but they have been listed in random order. Your job is to discover a sequence for these assertions based on the inverted pyramid. Ideally, your sequence should correspond to the one represented in the original story, but with less important pieces this may not always happen. Your sequence will be functional if you can justify it in terms of the inverted pyramid.

1. Group the assertions into blocks of related information by writing the assertion numbers in the appropriate blank spaces. Assume that the blocks of information represent, in rough form, the paragraphs of the article. Do not worry about transitions. Consider the assertions merely as separate items of information. NOTE: there are many more blanks than assertions. You are not required to use every space in each block (nor even to use all the blocks). Use as many as you need on the basis of the relationships you see among the assertions provided.

2. Briefly describe why you arranged the blocks (i.e., paragraphs) in the way you did. Describe only the sequence of the blocks, not the order of assertions within the blocks.

3. Select any one of the blocks and describe in detail your reasons for the sequence of assertions you established within that block.

SET OF ASSERTIONS

1. After such an operation, the human recipient would no longer be "himself" but would have the memory, intelligence, and personality of the brain donor.

2. The operation involves linking the windpipe and the veins and arteries of the recipient's body with the head of the donor.

3. Although Dr. White admits that it would be as easy to transplant a human head as it is to transplant a monkey's head, no human transplants are anticipated.

4. A Cleveland brain surgeon has performed eight head transplants on monkeys, one of which lived for thirty-six hours.

5. The operation, when performed on a human, would be called a "body transplant" and not a "brain transplant."

6. It is necessary to remove the head from the donor, Dr. White said, because it is impossible in a living animal to cut all the nerve connections between brain and body without removing the head.

7. Such an operation on a human would require social and governmental permission.

8. The head is not connected to the new body's nervous system.

9. The surgeon, Dr. Robert White, says that the purpose of this operation is to study the way the brain operates when isolated from the rest of the nervous system.

Group the assertions into blocks of related information by writing the assertion numbers in the appropriate blank spaces. Assume that Block I represents the first paragraph of a news story and that successive blocks represent successive paragraphs.

Using the inverted pyramid as a model, list in Block I the numbers of the most significant items, in Block II the numbers of less significant items, and so on, until you have accounted for every item.

Here is one possible sequence for the information:

BLOCK I	BLOCK II	BLOCK III	BLOCK IV
4	6	3	none
9	2	7	
	8	1	
		5	

The reasoning behind the sequence is this:

Block I tells the reader exactly what operation has been performed and the reason for it. It states what is significant about the operation. Block II explains what is involved in the operation and why it must be done the way it is. Block III includes some "human interest" information that might have been more important if there had been a serious suggestion of performing head transplants on humans. This information is not particularly significant since the article is specifically about experiments involving monkeys.

The reasoning behind the sequence of Block III is this:

The most important piece of information in this block is item 3 (no human transplants are anticipated): hence, that information comes first. Item 7 (the need for public approval) follows item 3, since it indicates the restrictions placed on anyone who might want to try a human transplant; that is, it indicates in part why no transplants are anticipated. Item 1 (the change in personality) follows item 7; it speculates about what would happen if such a transplant were performed. Item 5 (the name of the operation) modifies item 1.

Summary

Once you have a set of information and an organizing idea, determine where any given piece of information belongs within your statement. Then organize your information into a sequence that evolves from one assertion to the next until your statement is complete.

Recognizing that your reader's priorities are different from your own will always guide you in establishing a sequence. You use your reader's perspective to help you order your information. One example of how to use your reader's perspective to establish a functional sequence is the inverted pyramid.

The inverted pyramid is not the most comprehensive model of a functional sequence, but it does take into consideration the difference between the order in which the writer naturally perceives information and the order in which the reader perceives it.

Do You Understand the Concept of the Inverted Pyramid?

The following questions will aid you in summarizing what you have learned in this chapter.

How does language convey information, and what consequences does this have for the writer?

What does the inverted pyramid attempt to reconcile?

Describe the inverted pyramid:

Now Make Use of the Inverted-Pyramid Model

Working through the following writing situations will demonstrate your mastery of this chapter. Your instructor may suggest other situations or may encourage you to create your own.

You should be able to arrange sequences of information according to the model of the inverted pyramid.

Two different sets of assertions are given. Both sets are taken from actual news stories, but the assertions in each set have been listed here in random order. Your job is to discover, for each of these sets, a sequence that is based on the inverted pyramid. Ideally, your sequence in each case should correspond to the one represented in the original story. With less important pieces of information this may not always happen. Your sequence will be functional if you can justify it in terms of the inverted pyramid.

1. Group the assertions into blocks of related information by writing the assertion numbers in the appropriate blank spaces. Assume that the blocks of information represent, in rough form, the paragraphs of the article. Do not worry about transitions. Consider the assertions merely as separate items of information. NOTE: There are many more blank spaces than assertions. You are not required to use every space in each block (nor even to use all the blocks). Use as many as you need on the basis of the relationships you see among the assertions provided.

2. Briefly describe why you arranged the blocks (i.e., paragraphs) in the way you did. Describe only the sequence of blocks, not the order of assertions within the blocks.

3. Select any one of the blocks and describe in detail your reasons for the sequence of assertions you established within that block.

Set of Assertions 1:

1. School officials feel that many more children will participate in the lunch program when 45 cents will buy a hot meal, not a box lunch.

2. The city originally planned to begin serving hot lunches last spring.

3. None of the equipment can be purchased until the state gives the money to the city school system.

4. Only about twenty-four of the system's school children have chosen the box lunches over food brought from home.

5. The program became stalled because the state provided only a small part of the money the city requested.

6. The equipment includes steam tables, tables and chairs, sinks, and garbage disposals.

7. The long-delayed hot lunch program for the city schools may begin soon, if the state provides the necessary financial support.

8. Most pupils have displayed little interest in the cold lunches now offered.

9. The state funds, when they arrive, will be used to purchase the equipment necessary to prepare and serve the lunches.

Group the assertions into blocks of related information by writing the assertion numbers in the appropriate blanks. Assume that Block I represents the first paragraph of a news story and that successive blocks represent successive paragraphs.

Using the inverted pyramid as a model, list in Block I the numbers of the most significant items, in Block II the numbers of less significant items, and so on, until you have accounted for every item.

BLOCK I	BLOCK II	BLOCK III	BLOCK IV
_____	_____	_____	_____
_____	_____	_____	_____
_____	_____	_____	_____
_____	_____	_____	_____

Explain the sequence of blocks:

Explain the sequence of assertions in a particular block (choose one):

Set of Assertions 2:

1. Armstrong found that the lunar surface was "very, very fine grain," a "sandy surface."

2. Planting the flag did not make the moon America's territory. Under the treaty signed by eighty nations, the moon belongs to all human beings.

3. With millions throughout the world watching the black and white television pictures they beamed back, Armstrong and Aldrin planted the American flag and explored the gray, alien surface of rocks, hills, ridges, and dust that turned their blue space-boots cocoa-colored.

4. America's two moon pioneers completed man's first exploration of the lunar surface today and sealed themselves back in their spaceship Eagle for the hazardous voyage home.

5. They used specially designed scoops to gather rocks, dirt, and core samples from the surface.

6. The flight captured the imagination not only of the Americans but also of people around the world.

7. On Earth, 142 scientists from many different countries were waiting to study the samples to see if they will give any clue to the origin of the moon and the universe.

8. *Pravda* said, "The courageous cosmonauts have landed on the moon." But it gave bigger headlines to its still mysterious Luna 15, which remained in the lunar orbit.

9. History will mark the time as 10:56:20 P.M.

10. Television clearly showed Armstrong backing down a ladder on the lunar module and planting his left foot on the surface.

11. First the samples, like the astronauts, will have to spend twenty-one days in quarantine.

12. "That's one small step for man—one giant leap for mankind," Armstrong said.

Group the assertions into blocks of related information by writing the assertion numbers in the appropriate blank spaces. Assume that Block I represents the first paragraph of a news story and that successive blocks represent successive paragraphs.

Using the inverted pyramid as a model, list in Block I the numbers of the most significant items, in Block II the numbers of less significant items, and so on, until you have accounted for every item.

BLOCK I	BLOCK II	BLOCK III	BLOCK IV	BLOCK V
_____	_____	_____	_____	_____
_____	_____	_____	_____	_____
_____	_____	_____	_____	_____
_____	_____	_____	_____	_____

Explain the sequence of blocks:

Explain the sequence of assertions in a particular block (choose one):

12. Forecasting

Chapter 11 indicated that the inverted pyramid is a functional sequence that acknowledges the difference between the order in which the writer learns and the priorities of the reader. As writers, you can reconcile this difference by beginning any statement with an estimate of the significance of your information and an estimate of the sequence of that information.

Chapter 12 will focus on how you reveal to your reader your estimate of both the significance and the sequence of your information. You do this by forecasting. You forecast your tentative organizing idea and a tentative sequence of information.

The Dilemma of Functional Writing

Any functional writing situation presents you with a dilemma. When your reader begins to read, he or she wants to know something you are not yet sure of, namely, the significance of what you want to say. This dilemma can be resolved because an organizing idea evolves as you write.

As Chapter 3 explained, your organizing idea is not static; it grows or evolves as you develop your statement. It begins as a rough estimate of your destination. It becomes progressively clearer to you as you find relationships in the information that comprises your statement. Accordingly, you move from a tentative organizing idea about the significance of your information to a developed organizing idea about that significance.

Forecasting Your Tentative Organizing Idea

In sum, using the inverted pyramid you make a set of promises to the reader. Ideally, you would like to tell the reader exactly what you are going to say, but not knowing that, you settle for the next best thing. You make a tentative assertion about the significance of your information. Then you forecast approximately where you expect to arrive, and you state the limits of your subject matter.

By making a tentative assertion, you give your intended reader a sense of significance. You make a tentative declaration about the importance of your information, and you present it as a guide to what you are going to say. Then, as you write, you explore your organizing idea and give the reader progressively more evidence to support its development.

Readers are wholly dependent upon this sense of direction for completing their own process of learning about the writer's subject. As you saw in Part 2, any reader is both ignorant of the writer's organizing idea and impatient to find out about it. Readers will continue to read only if you assert your tentative organizing idea early in your statement. Readers do not expect to learn everything in the first paragraph, but they do need your estimate of the significance of the information you are communicating. They are willing to continue to read in order to learn the writer's developed organizing idea only if the writer forecasts it.

Forecasting Your Sequence

Suppose you want to write a statement broadly describing Darwin's theory of natural selection to a group of readers who are educated but who are not scientists. You already have a tentative idea about the significance of the theory, and you want to assert this significance. You also have a sense of relationship that can help you to arrange your information into categories or blocks of information.

You realize in a general way that there are possibly five different aspects to the theory; that is, your information falls into five categories. You do not know precisely how the five aspects of the theory affect each other, and your may not know precisely what you will do with the information you have arranged. Nevertheless, once you have a tentative assertion and a tentative plan for sequencing your information, you are ready to forecast for your reader. Your forecast must include a tentative organizing idea and a tentative sequence.

The following could serve as an opening paragraph that forecasts for your reader. (Some of the sentences have been separated for ease of reference.)

> Darwin's theory of natural selection explains the various processes of evolution. It explains what they are and also how they have worked over the centuries. The theory was highly controversial during the nineteenth century, but it is now accepted in most scientific circles as the best available answer to the mysteries of evolution.
>
> The theory can be divided into five distinct aspects or categories: (a) overproduction, (b) struggle for existence, (c) variation, (d) survival of the fittest, (e) origin of new species through inheritance of successful variations. These categories are interrelated and mutually dependent, but they can be distinguished for purposes of examination.

Notice the ways in which this paragraph forecasts both a tentative organizing idea and a tentative sequence.

The first two sentences state in basic terms the significance of Darwin's theory of natural selection. They show the reader the importance of whatever remarks will follow. They provide a context for evaluating the information to come.

The third sentence broadens the context. It suggests that the theory is pertinent, that it has scientific currency, and that it provides a reliable explanation of evolution.

These first three sentences assert the way the writer will finally evaluate Darwin's ideas later in the statement; they imply a tentative organizing idea for the statement. The last two sentences forecast a tentative sequence of what will follow.

The fourth sentence describes the five topics to be considered in the analysis of Darwin's theory. It tells the reader the specific kinds of information to expect and the order of their presentation. In other words, this sentence begins to establish a tentative sequence.

The fifth sentence gives the reader a glimpse of the way the writer will regard the five components of the sequence, that is, as interconnected natural processes.

If you were the writer, you could elaborate on these five sentences later in your statement. The point is, you have already described for the reader (1) what your tentative organizing idea is going to be and (2) how you are going to arrange your sequence for your reader.

A Forecast in Detail

You are writing a popular manual for amateur geologists. You want to describe those properties of rocks that are accessible to simple tests for determining particular rock specimens. Your readers have at best a general understanding of geological theory. They are not trained in the technical apparatus of the science. Their concern is strictly for Saturday afternoon field trips, not laboratory analysis.

You have accumulated the following information concerning the properties of rocks and the simple tests for identifying rock specimens. Notice that the information is fragmentary, just as it would be in the notes you might make for an actual statement. Note also that different items serve the writer in different ways. Item 7, for example, is a general statement; item 9 is a detail; item 4 is a writer's note to organize information in a certain way.

1. cleavage planes highly indicative of certain kinds of rock
2. color: a good hint to identity of a mineral
3. simple tests versus complicated tests
4. note: use properties of rocks to determine identity
5. structure versus surface appearance, chemistry versus common observation
6. resistance to scratching indicates hardness
7. rocks are primary documents of earth sciences
8. geologists use a scale of hardness for classifying rocks
9. when cobalt is found in corundum, the substance is bluish and called sapphire
10. when struck properly, minerals tend to cleave along characteristic lines
11. what does a geologist do?
12. "streak" is the color of a mineral when powdered by rubbing against unglazed porcelain
13. cleavage is the tendency of crystalline structures to break along definite planes depending on atomic structure and chemical bonds
14. rock hounds can often identify specimens by simple tests of visible characteristics
15. early man classified rocks mainly by their color

Given this set of information:

a. In the space provided list the categories or blocks of information that would be most appropriate for the first paragraph of a statement based on the set of information. Identify these categories with a word or a phrase.

b. Write an opening paragraph that forecasts your tentative organizing idea and your tentative sequence for that information.

Here are the categories of information that you plan to forecast. At this stage, no particular order is necessary.

identification and classification _____

surface appearance _____

chemical properties _____

kinds of tests _____

_____

_____

Here is a paragraph, based on these categories, that forecasts the writer's tentative organizing idea. (In reading this paragraph note the two things that are forecast: the tentative assertion and the tentative sequence.)

Rocks are the primary documents used in the earth sciences. The most essential business of a geologist is to identify and classify the many varieties of rocks that can be found in our environment. In order to determine the identity of a particular specimen, the geologist analyzes its physical properties. These properties may belong to its chemical make-up, for instance, atomic structure, or they may be part of its surface appearance, for instance, color or hardness. To evaluate these properties the geologist uses a number of tests, some complicated and available only in the lab, but others simple and available even in the field. The amateur rock hound can often identify a specimen solely on the basis of its surface characteristics and needs only the simplest tests to aid in evaluation. Let us look at these most common surface properties and at the tests anyone can use to assess them.

This paragraph is merely one way of organizing the items listed above. There are many possibilities, but the success of any variation depends on how well it forecasts both the tentative organizing idea and the tentative sequence of that information.

Summary

When you write you must reveal early in your statement an estimate of the significance of your information and the direction of your statement. You do this by forecasting. In your forecast, you include both a tentative organizing idea and a tentative sequence for your information. After you forecast, your reader will expect you to develop your organizing idea in the direction you have indicated.

Do You Understand the Concept of Forecasting?

The following questions will aid you in summarizing what you have learned in this chapter.

Any functional writing situation presents the writer with a dilemma. Explain the nature of this dilemma.

What feature of the organizing idea enables a writer to resolve the dilemma of functional writing?

What must a forecast include?

Now Use the Concept of Forecasting in Your Own Writing

Working through the following writing situations will demonstrate your mastery of this chapter. Your instructor may suggest other situations or encourage you to create your own.

You should be able to forecast a tentative organizing idea and a tentative sequence in any writing situation.

WRITING SITUATION 1

You are writing a simple introductory essay concerning the effects of certain fifteenth-century inventions on the development of European society. The essay is to be included in a textbook for children of grade school age.

Your readers are ten to twelve years old.

You have accumulated the following set of information concerning three inventions of the late Middle Ages and their effect on Europe in the early Renaissance. Notice that the information is fragmentary, just as it would be in the notes you might make for an actual statement.

A 1. influence of gunpowder on military tactics

D 2. both individual and society in general changed dramatically by advances in late medieval technology

B 3. sundial and hourglass inefficient time-keepers

C 4. after Gutenberg books could be printed cheaply and in quantity

A 5. gunpowder first discovered in China

D 6. three fifteenth-century inventions had profound effect on European life: clock, firearms, printing press

A 7. increase of violence in European cities

B 8. clock brought coordination to city life

D 9. these inventions meant a more dynamic society: warfare streamlined, communication easier, fast-paced city life encouraged over rural domesticity

C 10. availability of writing revolutionized European culture

C 11. paper-making introduced into Europe in thirteenth century

D 12. contrast between Middle Ages and Renaissance

A 13. development of firearms changed basic military unit from cavalry to infantry

C 14. low cost of paper encouraged profusion of diaries, letters, and business records

D 15. modern civilization dates from Renaissance

Given this set of information:

a. In the space provided list the categories or blocks of information that would be most appropriate for the first paragraph of a statement based on the set of information. Identify these categories with a word or a phrase.

_____

_____

_____

_____

_____

_____

b. Write an opening paragraph that forecasts your tentative organizing idea and your tentative sequence for that information.

Paragraph (continued):

You have just traveled to New Mexico and Arizona, and you have become concerned about the living conditions of the Navajo and Hopi
Indian people who live on reservations in that area. You have decided to
write to the Bureau of Indian Affairs to register your disapproval of the
situation and to recommend that the government take a more active role
in improving conditions on the Southwestern reservations.

Your reader is the director of the Bureau of Indian Affairs.

You have accumulated the following set of information about the Indian problem. Notice that the information is fragmentary, just as it would be in the notes you might make for an actual statement.

1. Southwestern population mainly on desert lands
2. federal government should assist in maintaining native cultural traditions separate from interference of white society
3. Indians forced to farm unproductive land
4. Indians poorly educated and poorly equipped to survive outside reservation
5. inadequacy of government assistance
6. treatment of Indians a bleak chapter of American history
7. commercial exploitation of Indians
8. Indians must have economic stability in order to become fully self-directing
9. kinds of possible governmental assistance
10. cultural traditions
11. living conditions need vast improvement
12. Sioux and Blackfoot live north of the Navajo and Hopi
13. educational services need expansion in order to solve both the cultural and the economic crises
14. moral obligation to American Indian

Given this set of information:

a. In the space provided list the categories or blocks of information that would be most appropriate for the first paragraph of a statement based on the set of information. Identify these categories with a word or a phrase.

_____

_____

_____

_____

_____

_____

b. Write an opening paragraph that forecasts your tentative organizing
   idea and your tentative sequence for that information.

Paragraph:

13. A System of Assertions

Chapter 12 described how you forecast in order to reassure your reader about what kind of statement to expect. You begin by declaring a tentative organizing idea and a tentative sequence of information. These assurances will tell your reader what to anticipate.

Your forecast will contain a number of assertions. This chapter will show you how to use the assertions in your forecast to generate new assertions that will extend your statement to the reader. You will be able to state your assertions successively, so that each assertion extends the assertions that it follows. When assertions are presented in progression, these declarations of relationship are the building-blocks of an argument.

What Is an Argument?

An argument is a line of reasoning; it is a logical progression from one assertion to another that implies both a direction and some eventual destination or conclusion. Popular usage has obscured this older, more accurate definition of "argument." The word is often assumed to mean nothing more than an aggressive way of stating an opinion. It is often limited to meaning merely "dispute." In its broad and basic sense, however, the term "argument" is defined as a pattern of declarations intended to establish a position. Specifically, an argument is a connected series of assertions supported and clarified by evidence.

To argue is to make reasoned choices among the many assertions that you could declare about your subject. You choose what to include and what to exclude, what to say first and what to say next, what to combine and what to separate. The assertions you choose to state should progressively clarify the significance of what you are saying. Any statement is an argument insofar as it contains a progressive series of assertions.

What About the Components of an Argument?

Arguments are composed of assertions: an assertion is the smallest unit of an argument. As you recall from Chapter 2, an assertion happens to be expressed in the form of a sentence, because nothing less than a sentence can assert a relationship. There is a distinction to be made, however. An assertion is a component of an argument, not because it is a sentence, but because it states a relationship.

This distinction between an assertion and a sentence is important. It is a distinction between a rhetorical entity and a linguistic entity. An assertion can be independent of any particular sentence. For example, here are three different sentences that convey the same assertion:

1. I had an alligator purse.
2. My purse was made of alligator hide.
3. Alligator hide was used to make my purse.

Moreover, because an assertion is a statement about a relationship or a number of relationships, the same sentence can convey several different assertions. Here is an example:

I lost my purse with my keys and my credit cards in it.

One assertion is explicit: "I lost my purse"; two others are implied in the sentence: "I lost my keys"; and "I lost my credit cards." Two other implied assertions about the contents of the purse are more deeply embedded in the sentence: "my keys were in my purse" and "my credit cards were in my purse."

As rhetorical entities, some assertions become organizing ideas depending on their function in any given argument. In any paragraph or sequence of paragraphs, the organizing idea is the most important assertion of relationships, and it has the same distinctive, logical properties as any other assertion. As you recall from Chapter 3, an organizing idea can be expressed in a sentence, although it is not the same as a sentence; it is a rhetorical entity.

Every paragraph is composed of many assertions. Together, these declarations of relationship develop an organizing idea. Any of the assertions in each paragraph may be explicit or implied, which is also true of the organizing idea. Together they form a system, a line of reasoning. The following paragraph is an example of a system of assertions, one of which is an organizing idea. The paragraph has six sentences; but there are at least twenty explicit assertions in this paragraph, and many more implied assertions are embedded in the sentences.

A substantial minority of today's population is gay. Many homosexuals are unaware of their membership in this significant minority and consequently go through much of their lives feeling miserable, sensing their alienation from the straight majority. Because these individuals know that society condemns their sexual preferences, they often choose to lead two separate lives: a straight life as their social facade, a gay life only among their friends. The alternative is to risk public ridicule, defamation of character, and even bodily injury. The gay community, in other words, suffers the same indignities, the same disenfranchisement, that other suppressed minority groups are forced to endure in this country. And these indignities will continue until gays unite and assert their collective claim to the rights and privileges they deserve.

The essential declaration in this paragraph, its organizing idea, can be expressed in the following sentence: "Only when homosexuals unite and insist on their rights will they be freed from the indignities they are presently forced to suffer." But this conclusion about the significance of the paragraph as a whole evolves by means of several other assertions that relate only parts of that significance.

An Argument Is a System of Assertions

As mentioned earlier, an assertion is the smallest unit of an argument. When you name all of the assertions in a single paragraph, you describe its argument. When you name the major assertions, or organizing ideas, of all the paragraphs in a given sequence, listing them in order, you describe the argument of that sequence.

With your knowledge of assertions, you can now state more precisely what an argument is and what it does. An argument is a system of assertions in which each declaration depends on others before and after it. An argument reveals a line of reasoning that points toward some conclusion or developed organizing idea. If you consider an argument as a structure, then assertions are its building-blocks. If you consider an argument as a line of reasoning, then assertions are points along that line. You evolve your statement by relating declarations through successive paragraphs until you have discovered a conclusion.

Using Your Forecast to Generate Assertions

Chapters 2 and 3 described how you make assertions about your subject as you write paragraphs. The process of making assertions is the same whether you are writing a single paragraph or a sequence of paragraphs.

When you write a sequence of paragraphs, however, you need to state a tentative idea about the assertions you might make in that sequence, and you need to state a tentative order for these assertions. In other words, you need to forecast a tentative organizing idea and a tentative sequence. You can then use your forecast as a guide in writing paragraphs about your subject. The guide is for both you and your reader.

Suppose you plan to write a statement about the subject "the violent use of guns." Your frame of reference acknowledges that problems can be solved only by dealing with their causes. Accordingly, you feel that some action should be taken on the misuse of guns. You realize that you need to find more information about your subject, and you gather the following items:

- right to handle guns
- heated family arguments
- not even hunters and collectors handle guns safely
- guns for protection
- availability of guns
- stolen guns
- children are innocent victims
- misuse of guns is a social problem
- inadequate preparation

You decide on the basis of this information that a tentative organizing idea for your statement might be: "It is time to consider what action should be taken by our society to deal with the violent use of guns."

Suppose your reader is the junior senator from your state. He has recently been the victim of armed robbery in his own home. Election time is drawing near. He must take a position about gun-control legislation, one of the major issues among his constituents. His implied question might be: "What do the voters think about gun-control?"

Now that you have a reader and a tentative organizing idea, your next task is to arrange your information into categories. These categories will become the aspects of the subject that you focus on. At this stage no particular order is necessary.

CATEGORIES OF INFORMATION

misuse of guns in the home   concern about gun abuse

mishandling of guns by hunters and collectors   criminal use of guns

Because you now have a tentative organizing idea and the main categories of information, you can write the first draft of your forecast. It might look like this

> It is understandable that many people are concerned about the availability of guns in our society. This availability, they argue, must be restricted in order to prevent violence and to insure public safety. There is considerable evidence that many acts of violence are related to guns. Thousands of people abuse the right to handle a gun every day: not only criminals, but also hunters and collectors, as well as other innocent people. It is time to consider what action should be taken by our society to deal with the violent use of guns.

Now that you have a first draft of your forecast, with a tentative organizing idea that anticipates a sequence, you can begin to make assertions about the categories of the information you plan to use. You do this by deciding what you want to say about any of these categories. Suppose

you decide to focus on "mishandling of guns by hunters and collectors."
You might decide to use these pieces of information:

- hunting accidents
- inadequate preparation
- not even hunters and collectors handle guns safely

Your first draft of the first paragraph about "mishandling of guns by hunters and collectors" might look like this:

> Hunters and collectors, themselves, are not safe from acts of violence related to guns. Each year during the hunting season, inexperienced hunters maim or kill other hunters or innocent bystanders who are mistaken for game. Many hunters or collectors, who are not adequately prepared for the privilege of owning guns, wound themselves, sometimes fatally, because they do not know how to clean them. There must be some way to convince hunters and collectors that the mishandling of guns can result in regrettable violence.

You can see that this paragraph makes many new assertions about your subject. Incidentally, there are many more assertions than sentences. For example, here are some of the assertions that writing these two paragraphs may have helped to generate. Any of them could now be used again in any way you wish. Notice how you would be generating new information simply by writing.

- Many people are concerned about the availability of guns in our society.
- It is understandable that many people are concerned about this availability.
- They argue that this availability must be restricted.
- This availability must be restricted in order to prevent violence.
- This availability must be restricted in order to insure public safety.
- Many acts of violence are related to guns.
- There is considerable evidence that many acts of violence are related to guns.
- Thousands of people abuse the right to handle a gun every day.

- Criminals abuse the right to handle a gun.
- Hunters abuse the right to handle a gun.
- Collectors abuse the right to handle a gun.
- Innocent people abuse the right to handle a gun.
- It is time to consider what action should be taken to deal with the violent use of guns.
- It is time to consider what action should be taken on this issue by our society.
- Hunters are not safe from acts of violence related to guns.
- Collectors are not safe from acts of violence related to guns.
- Inexperienced hunters maim or kill other hunters.
- Inexperienced hunters maim or kill innocent bystanders.
- These accidents happen during the hunting season.
- Hunters are mistaken for game.
- Innocent bystanders are mistaken for game.
- Hunters who are inadequately prepared wound themselves.
- Gun collectors who are inadequately prepared wound themselves.
- These wounds are sometimes fatal.
- These hunters do not know how to clean their own guns.
- These collectors do not know how to clean their own guns.
- There must be some way to convince hunters that mishandling of guns can result in regrettable violence.
- There must be some way to convince gun collectors that mishandling of guns can result in regrettable violence.

You could continue to make assertions by writing another paragraph about this category of information or about any other category of your information. You might find that some of your assertions could serve as organizing ideas for paragraphs. Others may have to be subordinated to more important assertions. Some assertions might generate new declarations that could provide materials for several paragraphs. You might even want to discard some of your assertions because they would take too much time to relate to the tentative organizing idea of your statement. Chapters 14 and 15 will show you how to use the assertions you make as building-blocks for your argument.

Summary

After you have gathered information and written a forecast for your reader, you are ready to make further assertions about your subject. With your forecast as a guide, you write paragraphs that cause you to generate new assertions about various categories of information. These assertions are declarations of relationships; they are the building-blocks of your argument. Any argument is a line of reasoning; it is a logical progression from one assertion to another that implies both a direction and some eventual destination.

Do You Understand the Concepts of Argument and Assertion?

The following questions will aid you in summarizing what you have learned in this chapter.

Using the concept of "choices," how would you define an argument?

What is the smallest unit of an argument?

How does an assertion differ from a sentence?

After you have written your forecast, how does it continue to serve you?

Now Generate Some Assertions of Your Own

Working through the following writing situations will demonstrate your mastery of this chapter. Your instructor may suggest other situations or may encourage you to create your own.

Given any subject, you should be able to forecast an argument, and you should be able to make assertions that will become the building-blocks of that argument.

Select two of the following subjects or choose two of your own:

Women's rights	Alcoholism
Television	Capital punishment
Ecology	Euthanasia

For each subject, choose a reader and suggest this reader's implied question, then gather information, assert a tentative organizing idea, state your categories of information, forecast your argument, write a forecast paragraph, and write another paragraph about any category of information. Then list seven or eight of the assertions you have generated.

Name _____ Instructor_____

SUBJECT 1
Reader's Frame of Reference and Implied Question:

Set of Information (ten to twelve items):

Tentative Organizing Idea:

Categories of Information:

_____

_____

_____

_____

_____

_____

Name _____ Instructor_____

Forecast Paragraph:

Paragraph on one Category of Information:

BUILDING AN ARGUMENT

Name ————————————————— Instructor—————————————————

Seven or eight of the assertions you have generated in the preceding
paragraphs:

SUBJECT 2
Reader's Frame of Reference and Implied Question:

Set of Information (ten to twelve items):

Name _____ Instructor_____

Tentative Organizing Idea:

Categories of Information:

_____

_____

_____

_____

_____

_____

Forecast Paragraph:

Name _____ Instructor_____

Paragraph on one Category of Information:

Seven or eight of the assertions you have genered in the preceding paragraphs:

BUILDING AN ARGUMENT

Name _____ Instructor_____

14. The Expanding Sequence

Chapter 13 introduced the concept of argument and expanded the concept of assertion. These concepts are essential to an understanding of the nature of sequence. An argument is a line of reasoning directed toward some destination. Assertions are the building-blocks of an argument. They reveal the writer's evolving line of reasoning to the reader. Assertions are what the writer and the reader use for their separate discoveries of some conclusion.

The Diminishing Sequence

You have already seen one variety of argument in Chapter 11, namely, the news story. Like any other argument, the news story involves the writer in a process of making choices about what to say and how to say it. The news story reveals a line of reasoning. It conveys a sequence of interrelated assertions.

The news story typifies the inverted pyramid. Specifically, it serves the need to forecast what you plan to say. It provides a way to get started that also accommodates your intended reader. This is its most important feature and its greatest advantage. The inverted pyramid has serious limitations, however. It is limited to a single function: it acknowledges the reader's frame of reference, but it is not flexible enough to allow full development of the writer's organizing idea. It is a diminishing sequence. This inflexibility is a basic shortcoming.

Here is why the diminishing sequence is inflexible. It moves from the most significant information (as the reader views it) to the least significant. Newspaper writers do not develop sequences in order to learn something new about a subject. Instead, they merely classify the information in their stories in a way that accommodates their readers' interests. The diminishing sequence has a function in a news story: it enables an editor to shorten the story if necessary without losing its news value; it also enables the casual reader to stop after the early paragraphs.

Typically, readers do not bother to read all the way through a news story because they realize that the information it contains becomes less important as they read down the column. The organizing idea can be found in the first paragraph or two. The rest of the story provides evidence for that organizing idea, but it does not provide a more developed conclusion about the significance of the subject.

Earlier assertions in a news story are always more important than later assertions. This feature characterizes the diminishing sequence. Here is an example of that sequence as it is often found in a news story. Notice that the declarations grow progressively less significant as you read down the list.

1. Massive frauds have been discovered in the city's nursing homes.
2. The central figure in the inquiry is John Smith.
3. Smith has not yet been available for questioning.
4. Investigations were made to discover the fraud in nursing homes.
5. Elvira Jones, new director of investigation, led the probes.
6. It was a horrible experience, Jones said later; she could not believe her eyes.

The most important assertion in this sequence is 1: massive frauds have been discovered in the city's nursing homes. This is the organizing idea of these assertions, the major declaration, and it could forecast any statement containing them. The forecast is so complete that it contains everything that follows. It not only includes the ideas that follow, but it also limits the statement of those ideas to the boundaries of the forecast. Assertions 2 through 6 elaborate and support 1, but they do not assume greater importance than 1. They clarify it, providing evidence, but they do not extend it.

The Expanding Sequence

The primary function of a news story is to transmit information as quickly and economically as possible. Its primary purpose is to satisfy the reader. In this sense, the news story is not typical of normal discourse, which satisfies the reader but also accommodates the writer's learning process.

You discover your developed conclusion by writing. Your earlier assertions generate realizations about what you can say; you realize that you can make assertions about your subject that are more developed and more precise. Your later assertions, therefore, are normally more significant than your earlier ones. You should know more, and therefore be able to say more, at the end of your statement than you could have said at the beginning.

A statement that represents a development of your understanding must therefore be an expanding sequence. This sequence is one in which later assertions are likely to be more important than earlier ones because they reflect your clearer awareness of what you are trying to say. An expanding sequence permits new discoveries. It allows for a conclusion that is more significant than any assertion that has led up to it. It enables a conclusion that represents your new awareness of the importance of your subject.

The advantage of the expanding sequence is evident: it enables you to learn as you go. But expansion raises a difficult question: how does the reader keep track of where the writer is heading? How can the expanding sequence accommodate the reader?

Remember from Chapter 11 the diagram that shows the advantages of the news model:

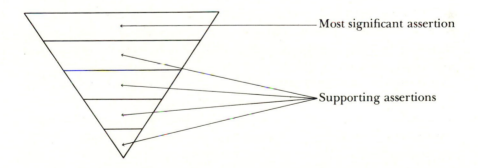

The reader knows at the start where the writer is going: everything later in the statement supports what has gone before. The sequence, therefore, is diminishing.

The expanding sequence, however, looks like this:

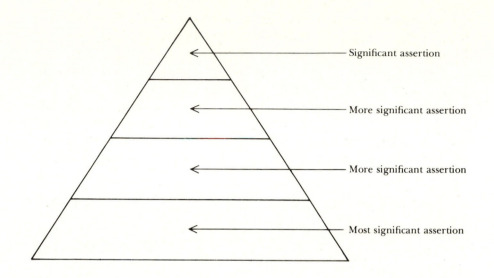

The question is: how can you gain the advantage of both these models at once; that is, how can you alert the reader to your own learning process? Can you satisfy both yourself and your reader as you write? Can you satisfy yourself by means of satisfying your reader?

The answer to all these questions is "yes." You can satisfy both yourself and your reader as you write. Better still, you can satisfy yourself by satisfying your reader. The answer lies in what you have learned about argument and assertion. Remember that any system of assertions progresses from one point to another. It has direction. Like a vector, it points somewhere. In this process one declaration leads to the next in a temporal sequence of related, interlocking, and often overlapping pieces of information.

You can forecast the system of assertions in an expanding sequence in the same way you forecast a diminishing sequence. In other words, you forecast the direction of your argument, your line of reasoning. There is one important difference, however: in an expanding sequence the forecast does not stop with your opening paragraph. You continue to forecast where you are going throughout the development of your statement. You show the reader how every new declaration relates to earlier ones. In other words, you keep the reader informed about the way you are expanding your system.

In an expanding sequence, then, forecasting becomes a means of development. You evolve your sequence through a process of continuous forecasting. You make successive choices about what to say next in a way that shows a connection with what you have already said. You therefore satisfy yourself by accommodating your reader.

Here is an illustration of an expanding sequence. The full process of forecasting cannot be revealed because the assertions in this sequence are not fully expanded into paragraphs. (In any case, the next chapter will discuss continuous forecasting as a means of development.) Notice the broadening significance of the following declarations. Notice, too, the logical relationship between any one assertion and those that precede it.

1. Massive frauds have been discovered in the city's nursing homes.
2. The extent of the fraud is truly horrifying.
3. Older persons live in filthy conditions, receive little care, and simply wait to die.
4. Society has left its senior citizens to die out of sight and out of mind.
5. Younger generations no longer assume the burden of caring for their parents, leaving them prey to unscrupulous nursing home operators.
6. The neglect of our older citizens is a dangerous sign of the deterioration of social responsibility in our culture.

Unlike the diminishing sequence you saw earlier, this argument evolves toward a conclusion in the last assertion (6). This final assertion is more comprehensive and more significant than anything expressed in earlier assertions. Later declarations do not merely modify the first one; instead, they evolve from the first one, each adding new significance, until the conclusion is reached.

This example illustrates the way in which writing is a learning process. The fact is that no assertion is definitive, no matter how conclusive it may sound to a listener or to a reader. To the speaker or writer every assertion conveys some suggestion of how it might be extended or expanded or refined. Try making an assertion about any subject, and see how easy it is to start a train of thought. In a writer's statement every assertion should represent unfinished business.

Simply by declaring a relationship you will perceive how it suggests other relationships. The words you use to state this relationship will signal other information you have already stored. The words you use convey references that suggest new relationships. In this way each assertion reveals to the writer the possibility of more to say. An expanding sequence of assertions is natural to the writer.

An expanding sequence of assertions is a function of the writer's learning process. Each assertion contains the suggestion of a new relationship. This new relationship is evolving in the writer's mind, but it has not yet happened for the reader. The writer's learning process need not confuse the reader if the writer will make each new relationship clear to the reader as soon as the writer becomes aware of it. (The next chapter will explain how to make these connections explicit for the reader.)

Recall the example of the fraud in the city's nursing homes. Each assertion evolves beyond the previous assertion. As far as the reader is concerned, there is no confusion about where the argument is leading even though the reader does not know its destination at the outset. The first prediction adequately forecasts the writer's concern for the poor care of the elderly; therefore, it predicts the direction of the argument.

Each assertion contains one part of the relationship that the next assertion declares. Each assertion is therefore an implicit forecast. Each succeeding declaration elaborates what has gone before but also adds something new, until the developed conclusion is reached. This conclusion is not merely that the elderly receive poor care; rather, it is that poor care of the elderly suggests the deterioration of social responsibility in our culture. The writer has discovered something new about the subject simply by being explicit about the implications in each previous assertion.

An Example of an Expanding Sequence

Suppose you decide to write a statement about change in American lifestyles. You are contemplating a change of residence from a suburb to the city, and you see this as a prospective change in your whole lifestyle. Your frame of reference leads you to feel that change is inevitable and that things usually work out for the better.

Suppose your reader is a real estate broker whose livelihood depends on the sale and rental of suburban property. This is the reader's implied question: "What is wrong with the suburbs?" or "Why should anyone move from here?" You wish to persuade this reader that your prospective move is in keeping with the times and not merely a personal preference.

To help you explain the subject, you have gathered the following information from various editorial statements you have read:

1. The city offers many different forms of entertainment.
2. Prices in any suburb are geared to a certain level of income.
3. The air is better in the suburbs.
4. You cannot walk to most places in the suburbs.
5. Without the need to commute the city dweller has more leisure time.
6. We have allowed cities to deteriorate.
7. The cost of home ownership in the suburbs is increasing at a phenomenal rate.
8. The city offers privacy.
9. The cities already have sewers.

From these assertions you form a tentative organizing idea: "We are returning to the city in order to cope with the realities of our environment." As you plan a sequence of what you want to say, you can see that your information falls into several categories:

disadvantages of the suburbs _____   possibilities of the city _____

disadvantages of the city _____   _____

_____   _____

Given your reader's frame of reference, that of a suburban real estate broker, you might then decide on this sequence for your set of assertions:

disadvantages of the city _____   _____

disadvantages of the suburbs _____   _____

possibilities of the city _____   _____

With this sequence and this tentative organizing idea you might write this forecast:

> Thirty years ago we moved to the suburbs for good reason. We were coping with the realities of our environment. The cities were becoming uninhabitable, and we wanted to escape them. But moving to the suburbs made us change our way of living. Now our lifestyle, still changing, needs a different kind of environment to support it, and it is time to move back to the city.

This forecast states a tentative organizing idea, and it predicts a sequence by which you will deal with the categories of information you have gathered. In doing this much it also does more. It makes several assertions that were not anticipated in the original planning. These assertions concern the relationship between one's lifestyle and one's environment. Even as you start to write, your awareness of your subject will start to grow.

Here is one way these new assertions might help you to develop another paragraph: specifically, a paragraph about the disadvantages of the city.

> The suburbs were once our hope for recapturing what we had lost in the city: fresh air, space to move around in, and relative security and protection for our normal activities. Even as we sought these values in the city, we allowed the deterioration of the environment that supported them. In time the urban environment contradicted the lifestyle that we sought.

Notice that this paragraph suggests another assertion, namely, the declaration of some kind of relationship between "lifestyle" and "values." It is likely to come up again in the discussion of the next category of information: the disadvantages of the suburbs.

> For a while, the new suburban environment supported our values, but this was only temporary. We spread out in larger homes, but the cost of homes increased at a phenomenal rate. We had space to move around in, but our moving around required a certain level of income. If our income was below this level, we could not afford what we valued.

Notice that writing about this category of information has generated some new assertions that extend the scope of the paragraph beyond what was originally anticipated: specifically, relationships between costs and benefits. Again you might expect that these new assertions will influence what you write next. The final category in the forecast concerns the possibilities of the city. Here is how it might develop:

> There is nothing new about our values. We still want privacy and space to move around in. We still want to thrive in our environment and not be limited by it. For these reasons we should consider living in the city again. We can sell our cars and walk. We can sell our suburban real estate and avoid the cost of home improvements. We do not need to suffer new costs and assessments, because the cities already have sewers and shopping centers. We can purchase privacy with our rent, and we can indulge in all of the forms of leisure and cultural enrichment that a city offers to all its citizens, no matter what their family status or their income. Given the possibilities of the urban environment, we cannot afford not to escape to the city.

Rereading this sequence of paragraphs about change in American lifestyles, you can see how each cluster of assertions has provided the writer with clues for extending and developing the tentative organizing idea. Every assertion provides some new information that the writer could use in a later assertion. Assertions breed more assertions, which is another way of saying that writing is a learning process.

Summary

The news story, which typifies the diminishing sequence, is one variety of argument. This inverted pyramid, however, has serious limitations. It acknowledges the reader's frame of reference, but it is not flexible enough to allow full development of your organizing idea. In order to develop your organizing idea, you must allow an expanding sequence to occur. This sequence permits new discoveries. It allows for a conclusion that is more significant than any assertion that leads up to it. This conclusion represents your new awareness of the importance of your subject.

Do You Understand the Concept of an Expanding Sequence?

The following questions will aid you in summarizing what you have learned in this chapter.

Can you explain why the diminishing sequence is inflexible?

What are the characteristics of an expanding sequence?

.

What is the principal advantage of an expanding sequence?

How does forecasting in an expanding sequence differ from forecasting in a diminishing sequence?

Now Create Some Expanding Sequences of Your Own

Working through the following writing situations will demonstrate your mastery of this chapter. Your instructor may suggest other situations or encourage you to create your own.

You should be able to arrange assertions into a sequence. You should also be able to build an argument following that sequence. Your argument should evolve as an expanding sequence of assertions.

Two sets of assertions have been provided below. The assertions in each set are all related to the same subject but are listed here in random order. Choose one of the sets and perform the following operations:

1. Read through the set of assertions and decide on a tentative organizing idea; write it in the space provided.

2. Select a reader and state the reader's implied question.

3. List the categories of your information.

4. Find a new sequence for the set of assertions using your tentative organizing idea as the first assertion in the sequence.

5. Find four new assertions that relate to the assertions in the original set and write them in the spaces provided.

6. Find a new sequence for the entire set of assertions (including the four you have just derived) using your tentative organizing idea in the sequence. (As you revise your sequence, you may find it necessary to revise your tentative organizing idea as well; revise it if necessary.)

7. Expand each assertion into a paragraph so that the initial system of assertions becomes an argument. You are expected to include, as your opening paragraph, a forecast of the argument you intend to present.

Set of Assertions 1:

1. Television commercials consistently represent women as wives, mothers, or housekeepers.

2. Advertisements in general audience magazines rarely represent blacks as authority figures.

3. Advertising rarely pictures a person in radical roles.

4. Men and women together in magazine ads are usually depicted in a romantic situation.

Set of Assertions 2:

1. Women who work for men normally have to overcome a patronizing attitude.

2. Generally women have the same managerial qualities as men.

3. Federal equal employment legislation has reshaped public opinion about women's roles in society.

4. Any woman in business contradicts one of the conventional assumptions about women.

Tentative Organizing Idea:

Reader and Reader's Implied Question:

Categories of Information:

_____

_____

_____

_____

_____

_____

Sequence of Assertions:

T.O.I.   (Tentative Organizing Idea)

____

____

____

____

Supplementary Set of Assertions:

5.

6.

7.

8.

Revised Sequence of Assertions:

T.O.I.   (Tentative Organizing Idea)

_____

_____

_____

_____

_____

_____

_____

_____

Argument:

Name _____ Instructor_____

Argument (continued): ....

BUILDING AN ARGUMENT

Name _____ Instructor _____

15. Continuous Forecasting

Chapter 14 explained that an expanding sequence has certain advantages over a diminishing sequence. Specifically, it shows how a writer can discover new significance by relating consecutive assertions until a developed conclusion reveals itself. This chapter also indicated that continuous forecasting is the most important feature in the writer's process of developing an argument.

How Does Continuous Forecasting Work in Developing an Argument?

What you forecast about a sequence is your best estimate of the relationships you intend to establish among your assertions. A sequence has direction. Your initial forecast gives the reader a sense of that direction. A sequence also entails an organized movement from one assertion to the next. As you write, therefore, you continue to forecast where you are going by telling your reader how every new assertion relates to those preceding. Stating that relationship is what advances your line of reasoning.

You advance your line of reasoning through the choices you make about selection and organization. Writing is a continuous process of choosing what to say next. And you choose what to say next by comparing what you have said already with what you want to say in your statement as a whole. Evaluating your system of assertions as it evolves enables you to discover new assertions. It also enables you to associate them with the context you are developing.

To help with this continuous evaluation of your context, you can ask yourself a question: "How does what I have said relate to what I want to say?" Asking this question will help to slow down the process of making choices; it will make you more self-conscious, and therefore more accurate, about the decisions you naturally make when you write.

This process of evaluation benefits both you and your reader. When you focus your attention on the logic of your choices, you clarify those choices for your reader. Conversely, as you strive to show your reader the connections among successive assertions, you make those connections clearer to yourself. When you reveal the relationship between one assertion and another, you forecast the direction of your argument. By revealing the pattern in your line of reasoning, as you learn about it, both you and your reader can anticipate new assertions that follow from the implications of those preceding.

The process is the same whether you are writing an individual paragraph or a sequence of paragraphs. You write successive sentences to indicate the direction of your paragraph. You write successive paragraphs to indicate the direction of your entire line of reasoning. You look backward and forward at the same time, always insuring that what you have said relates to what you want to say.

The reason for this similarity in the process of forecast and development is that paragraphs and paragraph sequences have the same essential characteristics. A paragraph is made up of assertions that are interrelated to form a system. It also has an organizing idea that is comprehensive: it states or implies the significance of that system. Each sentence in the paragraph is a reasonable guess about the connections between assertions already stated and assertions not yet stated. This is why a paragraph is said to evolve. The promise of its evolution is what the writer forecasts to his reader in every sentence.

The same is true of a sequence of paragraphs. Each paragraph in the sequence has an organizing idea. When the organizing ideas of all the paragraphs are listed in order, the result is a system of interrelated major assertions. The line of reasoning in a sequence of paragraphs is defined by the sequence of the organizing ideas of its paragraphs. As you write successive paragraphs, you show how each major assertion relates to those preceding. Stating this relationship constitutes an estimate of the importance of what is still to come. The stated relationship anticipates future assertions by revealing implications of earlier ones. Therefore, it reveals and also extends the writer's line of reasoning.

It is important to remember that forecasting is not merely a way to begin an argument; it is also a way to develop that argument. You advance your line of reasoning by continually evaluating the significance of the assertions you are relating. The process of evaluation is what generates news assertions. Letting your reader in on the process benefits not only the reader. It benefits you, too. The effort to reveal new relationships is what enables you to discover the full significance of those relationships for yourself.

When Is an Argument Coherent?

The coherence of an argument depends on the logic of its system of assertions. An argument is coherent to the degree that its sequence is self-evident. Each assertion in the argument must be relevant to its context; that is, it must be consistent with the other assertions surrounding it. A reader must be able to see how each assertion follows from assertions that have come before it and leads to those that come after. A coherent argument reveals its own structure. It reveals its own internal consistency by showing how its assertions are related.

Here is an example of sequential logic. Consider this set of information: "2, 4, 6, 8, 10." As you scan it, you become aware of the coherence of the set. It reveals its principle of relationship. Each number relates to the whole context because it is consistent with the other numbers surrounding it. Each number relates to the number before it by an increment of $+2$. The system reveals its own sequential logic because the relationships among its own constituents are apparent. It creates an expectation of an interval of 2 and then fulfills that expectation. The system is coherent, therefore, because its sequential logic is self-evident.

Now consider this set of numbers: "2, 4, 6, 3, 14." This set is not a system because its sequential logic is not self-evident. The set establishes an expected interval between numbers and then contradicts that interval. It fails to reveal a principle of relationship; therefore, it is incoherent.

The analogy to writing is clear. To develop a coherent argument the writer must reveal the sequential logic of a system of assertions, a line of reasoning. If readers cannot see a relationship between any given assertion and the assertions that surround it, they will not recognize the sequential logic of an argument. If the argument reveals no sequential logic, it is incoherent.

Continuous forecasting insures that the writer's argument preserves a sequential logic. It shows the reader how any assertion relates to its context. Continuous forecasting, then, is the way a writer achieves coherence.

How Do You Construct a Coherent Argument?

You can develop a coherent argument by recognizing the fact that any choice determines the kinds of choices that follow it. Because a written statement is linear, the choices you make in earlier sentences and paragraphs of your statement always affect the choices you can make later. In some ways your later choices are limited, and in some ways they are expanded. But in any case each assertion will be influenced by those that have preceded it.

This fact about successive choices is true of any linear system. If you fail to reconcile your later choices with those you have already made, you contradict the expectations you have already established in your reader. You interrupt the sequential logic of your statement; you fracture the interdependent relationship of its parts. To avoid such fractures and to preserve the coherence of your argument, you must insure that any piece of information is consistent with its context, that is, with the assertions that surround it. You must insure this consistency whether the context is a single sentence, a paragraph, or a sequence of paragraphs.

Consider the following set of assertions as an example. Does the set represent a coherent system as it stands? Do successive assertions forecast their relevance to what comes later by showing their relationship to what has come before?

1. Energy needs are increasing yearly by staggering degrees.
2. Nuclear power is dangerous and unpredictable.
3. Conservationists are fighting industry over water pollution.
4. Further use of available fossil fuels is becoming expensive and environmentally damaging.
5. Many new hospitals must be built in the coming decade.

6. The world is in serious danger of running out of energy.

7. Solar energy is the best alternative power source for the twenty-first century.

Each of these assertions makes sense by itself, but the set as a whole is not coherent. The relationships among assertions should be evident, but they are not. The set lacks sequential logic and is therefore incoherent. Imagine these assertions expanded into paragraphs. The sequence of paragraphs would reveal no line of reasoning.

What, for example, is the logical connection between "energy needs are increasing" and "nuclear power is dangerous"? The two assertions are going in different directions; they communicate fundamentally different kinds of information. The first assertion raises a certain kind of expectation in the reader's mind that is not fulfilled by the assertion that follows it. Since the second assertion does not extend or modify or develop the implications of the first assertion in any useful way, the two do not form a coherent sequence: their sequential logic is not self-evident.

Consider the association of assertion 6, the danger of running out of energy, and assertion 7, solar energy is the best alternative. In one sense, assertion 7 does follow: it suggests a possible source of energy, given the fact that the world is suffering from an energy shortage. But is the leap of reasoning justifiable? How does the mere fact of the world's energy shortage demonstrate that solar energy is the best answer to the problem? Clearly, other assertions must come between 6 and 7 before the two can be related. In this instance as well, therefore, the set of assertions lacks sequential logic.

How would you make this set coherent? To write a statement about the energy shortage, using these assertions, you would need to establish relationships among the assertions. Specifically, you would need to build a sequence that reveals how any one assertion relates to the assertions that precede it. You would also have to reject any assertion that could not be related in this way. Assertion 3, about water pollution, and assertion 5, about new hospitals, might not relate effectively to the other assertions. If so, they should be omitted from your sequence.

You can easily organize assertions into a coherent sequence. Choose any assertion from the set to begin your argument. Then find a second assertion that you think can be logically related to it. Then find a third assertion that relates to the sequence of the first two, and so on, through the set. As you expand each assertion to a paragraph, you forecast its significance in terms of your argument as a whole, and you also argue how and why it relates to the assertions that have come before. The coherence of your argument ultimately depends on how well you develop your assertions into full paragraphs that support one another and that reveal your line of reasoning.

An Illustration of Building an Argument

A set of assertions has been provided below. The statements are all related to the same subject but are listed here in random order.

1. Read through the set and decide on a tentative organizing idea; write it in the space provided.

2. Select a reader and suggest the reader's implied question.

3. List the categories of your information.

4. Find a new sequence for the set of assertions using your tentative organizing idea as the first sentence in the sequence.

5. Find four new assertions that relate to the assertions in the original set and write them in the spaces provided.

6. Find a new sequence for the entire set of assertions (including the four you have just derived) using your tentative organizing idea as the first sentence in the sequence. As you revise your sequence, you may find it necessary to revise your tentative organizing idea as well; revise it if necessary.

7. Expand each assertion into a paragraph so that the initial system of assertions becomes an argument. You are expected to include, as your opening paragraph, a forecast of the argument you intend to present. And you should use continuous forecasting throughout your statement in order to show how each assertion in your argument relates to the context that precedes it.

SET OF ASSERTIONS
1. The educational dilemma is not merely economic; it runs deep in the American system of values.

2. Adequate facilities and qualified teachers are provided to children from wealthy homes, while inadequate facilities and unqualified teachers are usually provided to children from poor homes.

3. Recent analysis of the sociopolitical history of the public schools indicates that they have been essentially a middle-class instrument used to "Americanize" the people they teach.

4. Shortcomings in urban schools have often been attributed simply to lack of funds.

A TENTATIVE ORGANIZING IDEA
The quality of education seems to vary considerably between urban and suburban schools, but the causes are complex and the cure will be difficult to find.

READER AND READER'S IMPLIED QUESTION
Suppose the reader is a local taxpayer. This reader's implied question could be: "What is the problem?" or "How serious is this problem?"

CATEGORIES OF INFORMATION

variations among schools _____   _____

complex causes _____   _____

crises defined _____   _____

A POSSIBLE SEQUENCE OF ASSERTIONS
(which represents your evolving strategy for building your argument)

T.O.I.   (Tentative Organizing Idea)

2 _____

4 _____

1 _____

3 _____

SUPPLEMENTARY SET OF ASSERTIONS
(that you would generate in order to fill in the gaps between assertions
you have already placed in sequence)

5. Young adults, particularly black urban school children, are
   seeking their own identities and do not choose to be flimsy caricatures of the American middle class.

6. The major reason for shortcomings in urban schools is the fact
   that school boards the country over are dominated by business
   and professional people who live in the suburbs and represent the
   middle class.

7. Economists maintain that there is just not enough money available to finance all of the urban schools.

8. When social and political institutions no longer operate in line
   with the values and hopes of particular groups, those groups will
   become alienated from them.

REVISED SEQUENCE OF ASSERTIONS
(representing your fully developed strategy for evolving your argument)

T.O.I.

2
___

4
___

7
___

1
___

3
___

6
___

5
___

8
___

(T.O.I.) The quality of education seems to vary considerably between urban and suburban schools. Unfortunately, the causes are complex and the cure may be difficult to find. Let us briefly consider some of those causes in order to assess our chances for solving the present crisis in American education.

2. Nearly everyone admits that children in the poorer urban schools do not fare as well as their suburban counterparts. Adequate facilities and qualified teachers are provided to children from wealthy homes, while inadequate facilities and unqualified teachers are usually provided to children from poorer homes.

4. The evident shortcomings in urban schools have often been attributed simply to lack of funds. The state legislature has argued, for example, that funds are limited in every school system, urban and suburban alike, but that the urban schools have many more problems so that they are not served proportionately by the funds they are allotted.

7. Many economists support this claim, arguing that, if more money were allocated to the urban systems, the quality of the facilities and the instruction would be certain to improve. Unfortunately, they add, the money is simply not available: hence, disadvantaged children remain disadvantaged.

1. It is important to realize, however, that the educational dilemma we are facing is far more than an economic problem. It runs deep in the American system of values, and any long-range solution will have to take into account the subtle attitudes that underlie and influence our approach to educational issues.

3. Recent analysis of the sociopolitical history of the public schools indicates that they have been essentially a middle-class instrument used to "Americanize" the people they presumed to educate. The public schools assume that their function is to certify for the young what is "right," what is "customary," what is "expected," and what is "wrong," in order to impose conformity on American society.

6. Probably the major reason for shortcomings in the urban schools is the fact that school boards the country over are dominated by business and professional people who live in the suburbs and represent the middle class. These school boards do not merely allocate funds. They also rule on what ideas will be taught, what texts will be used to teach them, how instructors will go about their teaching, and related matters, all reinforcing the system of values sustained by the middle class.

5. Many young people today are resisting this imposition of middle-class values on their own emerging individual and social identity. Black urban school children in particular have no interest in becoming caricatures of a social class to which they have never belonged and from which they have nothing to gain.

8. The essence of the crisis is this: when social and political institutions no longer operate in line with the values and hopes of particular groups, those institutions will be considered illegitimate, and the groups will become alienated from them. This is exactly what has happened in the urban schools. The poorer, inner-city children who attend these schools resist the prepackaged instruction they receive from well-meaning but naive middle-class teachers, and the quality of their educational experience inevitably deteriorates.

The statement you have just read is not complete. Because it contains an argument, it also implies a conclusion, a final assertion that follows from all the assertions that have come before. For the present, you can probably see how this statement has evolved (by means of a chain of interrelated assertions) to a point where a developed conclusion can be discovered. In Chapter 17 you will learn about how to write a developed conclusion.

Summary

Any argument has direction; it entails an organized movement from one assertion to the next. You forecast your argument by estimating the relationships you intend to establish among your assertions. This initial forecast gives both you and your reader a sense of direction.

As you develop your argument, you continue to forecast its direction by revealing the relationship between one assertion and another. By revealing the pattern in your line of reasoning, as you learn it, you can anticipate new assertions that follow from the implications of those preceding. The effort you make to reveal new relationships to your reader enables both you and your reader to discover the full significance of those relationships.

Do You Understand How to Build an Argument?

The following questions will aid you in summarizing what you have learned in this chapter.

You develop the argument of an expanding sequence by a process of continuous forecasting. What exactly do you forecast in each succeeding paragraph?

What two things does continuous forecasting enable you to do?

What questions can you ask yourself as an aid to making choices about what to say next?

How does the process of evaluation and continuous forecasting benefit both you and your reader?

When is an argument coherent?

What fact about the choice of any assertion must a writer recognize in order to develop a coherent argument?

Now Build Your Own Coherent Argument

Working through the following writing situations will demonstrate your mastery of this chapter. Your instructor may suggest other situations or encourage you to create your own.

You should be able to build a coherent system of assertions from any set of information, and you should be able to develop a paragraph sequence that incorporates the system.

Two sets of assertions have been provided below. The statements in each set are all related to the same subject but are listed here in random order. Choose one of the sets and perform the following operations:

1. Read through the set and decide on a tentative organizing idea; write it in the space provided.

2. Select a reader and suggest the reader's implied question.

3. List the categories of your information.

4. Find a new sequence for the set of assertions using your tentative organizing idea as the first sentence in the new sequence.

5. Find four new assertions that relate to the assertions in the original set and write them in the spaces provided. (Modify your categories of information if you wish.)

6. Find a new sequence for the entire set of assertions (including the four you have just derived) using your tentative organizing idea as the first sentence in the sequence. As you revise your sequence, you may find it necessary to revise your tentative organizing idea as well; revise it if necessary.

7. Expand each assertion into a paragraph so that the initial system of assertions becomes an argument. You are expected to include, as your opening paragraph, a forecast of the argument you intend to present. And you should use continuous forecasting throughout your statement in order to show how each assertion in your argument relates to the context that precedes it.

Set of Assertions:

1. Many doctors establish lucrative private practices in wealthy communities, while all too few are willing to accept the low pay and poor working conditions of inner-city hospitals.

2. Many claims have recently been made against the medical profession.

3. The American Medical Association has consistently opposed socialized medicine, some believe, because it would reduce the fees doctors customarily receive for their services.

4. Doctors have an obligation to cure the sick, wherever the sick may be, whatever they can afford to pay.

Set of Assertions:

1. National parks belong to the public and should be available for the public's use without restriction.

2. Foolish and careless campers are by far the most serious threat to the survival of our wilderness and wildlife preserves.

3. Our national parks provide one of the few escapes modern Americans have from the noise, smoke, and turmoil of the cities.

4. Overuse of some of our national parks has resulted in damage to the ecological balance of our last remaining wilderness areas.

(Choose one of these sets)

Name _____ Instructor_____

Tentative Organizing Idea:

Reader and Reader's Implied Question:

Categories of Information:

_____

_____

_____

_____

_____

_____

T.O.I.

____

____

____

____

Supplementary Set of Assertions:

5.

Name _____ Instructor_____

6.

7.

8.

Revised Sequence of Assertions (modify your categories of information
if you wish):

T.O.I.

_____

_____

_____

_____

_____

_____

_____

_____

Name _____ Instructor _____

Argument:

Argument (continued).

Name _____ Instructor_____

16. Review of Part 3

This chapter will serve as a review of the concepts you worked with in Part 3: especially functional sequence, forecasting, assertion, and argument. You should be familiar with these concepts and be able to use them as you write.

What Part 3 Indicates about Writing

Part 3 describes the nature of argument and the importance of forecasting as an effective means of communicating. An argument is a sequence of assertions. The writer's process of evolving an argument is the reverse of the reader's process of understanding it. Before evaluating the writer's sequence of assertions, the reader must know the direction of that argument and something about its significance. Therefore, the writer must forecast an organizing idea at the outset and continue to forecast its development with successive assertions.

The process of forecasting remains the same for a diminishing sequence or an expanding sequence, except that you continue to forecast an expanding sequence. The diminishing sequence, typified by news stories, is informative for the reader but restricting for the writer. It offers less freedom to explore a subject and thereby to learn something new about it. The expanding sequence, on the other hand, increases the writer's capacity to learn about a subject while accommodating the reader's need to know what the writer has learned. The expanding sequence, therefore, is ultimately more beneficial to both writer and reader; it enables them both to make discoveries.

The Essential Concepts of Part 3

Inversion is the process of changing one sequence into another. Specifically, the writer chooses a sequence that corresponds to the reader's priorities. The writer's natural process is to discover the significance of information by making assertions about it, but the reader needs some sense of this significance to begin with. The reader needs to know something about the writer's conclusion before understanding or evaluating the relevance of any single assertion. A **functional sequence,** therefore, is an inversion of the writer's natural movement toward a conclusion in order to accommodate the reader's need to anticipate that conclusion.

A **forecast** initiates the inversion of the writer's learning process to accommodate the reader's priorities. It is the writer's best guess about the significance of the information to follow, even before the writer has become fully aware of that significance. A forecast is a statement about the writer's line of reasoning. It is an estimate about the relevance of any particular assertion to the significance of the writer's argument as a whole.

Initially, the writer forecasts a tentative organizing idea as well as the direction of the argument. Then the writer explores the relationships among the assertions of the argument and forecasts progressively more accurate estimates of its conclusion. The writer continues to show the reader how each assertion relates to its context and then shows how the context as a whole implies still more assertions to come. This pattern of increasingly more accurate forecasts helps the reader to cope with the writer's developing line of reasoning. It also helps the writer to clarify the significance of that line of reasoning.

An **argument** is a system of assertions, where each assertion depends on other assertions before and after it. In other words, an argument is a line of reasoning. It is a directed movement from one idea to another, leading to some conclusion. Nearly all written statements characteristically develop arguments through successive and mutually dependent assertions until some conclusion reveals itself. The conclusion of an argument is the completion of the writer's learning process.

An **assertion** is the smallest unit of an argument. It states a connection. It declares a relationship among pieces of information. An assertion can be expressed as a single sentence, but it is not the same as a sentence. An assertion is a rhetorical entity, while the sentence is a linguistic entity.

Organizing ideas are always assertions, although not all assertions are organizing ideas. An organizing idea relates the sentences of a paragraph or a sequence of paragraphs; it is therefore the most important assertion in that paragraph or that sequence. Any statement will also contain other assertions that support the evolving organizing idea.

A system of assertions becomes a context. Any single assertion relates to this context when it is consistent with the assertions surrounding it. The coherence of an argument depends on the degree to which its logic is self-evident. The argument develops through a succession of assertions, each related to those that have come before. The system is coherent, therefore, to the extent that it reveals to any reader the interrelationships among its assertions.

Earlier assertions in an argument restrict the kinds of assertions that can follow, but they do not restrict the number of assertions. In fact, later assertions normally expand the significance of an argument by extending its chain of reasoning. In any case, the relationships among these assertions must be revealed if the argument is to be coherent.

Understanding the concepts of Part 3 is necessary to understanding the concepts of later chapters. If you are not certain about their meaning or their purpose, you may wish to consult your instructor before going on. As you grow familiar with the writing process, you can learn to recognize your own natural writing habits. You strengthen these habits by exercising them in different ways in different situations, and you thereby gain confidence in your ability to use them in any writing situation.

An Illustration of the Concepts of Part 3

Following is a completion of the statement included in Chapter 13, "A System of Assertions." You may recall that the subject of the statement is "the violent use of guns." In that chapter, you worked with this tentative organizing idea: "It is time to consider what action should be taken by our society to deal with the violent use of guns."

You recall that your reader is the junior senator from your state. He has recently been the victim of armed robbery in his own home. Election time is drawing near; he must take a position about gun-control legislation, one of the major issues among his constituents. As you recall, his implied question might be: "What do the voters think about gun-control?"

You recall that your supposed statement begins this way:

It is understandable that many people are concerned about the availability of guns in our society. This availability, they argue, must be restricted in order to prevent violence and to insure public safety. There is considerable evidence that many acts of violence are related to guns. Thousands of people abuse the right to handle a gun every day: not only criminals, but also hunters and collectors, as well as other innocent people. It is time to consider what action should be taken by our society to deal with the violent use of guns.

Your forecast includes your tentative organizing idea that action should be taken by our society to deal with the violent use of guns. It also anticipates your reader's priorities by stating a tentative sequence: first the abuse of the right to handle a gun by criminals, then by hunters and collectors, as well as other innocent people.

You might continue your statement this way:

Criminals have very little difficulty obtaining the guns they need. They find it relatively easy to purchase them. Often, the guns they use are stolen from the homes of collectors or hunters. Because guns are so readily available, many acts of violence are committed against innocent victims who deserve to be protected.

You have now developed the first aspect of your tentative sequence: the criminal use of guns. You have developed your organizing idea by suggesting that innocent victims need protection. You have also sustained the relationship you established earlier between guns and violence.

Suppose you continue to develop your argument:

Hunters and collectors, themselves, are not safe from acts of violence related to guns. Each year during the hunting season, inexperienced hunters maim or kill other hunters or innocent bystanders who are mistaken for game. Many hunters or collectors, who are not adequately prepared for the privilege of owning guns, wound themselves, sometimes fatally, because they do not know how to clean them. There must be some way to convince hunters and collectors that the mishandling of guns can result in regrettable violence.

You have now developed the second category of your sequence: the mishandling of guns by hunters and collectors. You have maintained the connection between guns and violence. You have also developed your organizing idea by suggesting that there must be some way to convince gun users, before they cause violence, that a gun may be a dangerous weapon.

Now suppose you develop the third category of your sequence, misuse of guns by other persons:

> Even more horrifying than the violence that criminals, hunters, and collectors inflict on innocent people by their irresponsible handling of guns are the gun-related incidents that occur in the home. Children are often seriously or fatally harmed by guns that their parents use for hunting or protection. There is also a very real danger that a heated family argument may lead to an intentional crime. In fact, violence is a condition that is always possible, and guns simply make it easier to occur.

In continuing this statement, you have further developed your equation of guns with violence. By discussing children, the family, and the home, you have provided more evidence for your organizing idea, namely, that it is time to consider what action should be taken.

Here would be an appropriate conclusion from the assertions already stated:

> The misuse of guns by criminals, by hunters and collectors, and even by innocent victims reveals that we must direct our energies toward an analysis of the many ways in which violence is manifested in our society. Guns are only one visible manifestation of this violence. The legislation of gun use will no more protect us from violence than the legislation of automobile use has protected us from violence on the highway. We need to analyze the causes of violence, intentional or unintentional. Only then can we institute programs that will deal with the causes of violence, not its manifestations, and that will help us to protect ourselves, by education, from unintentional violence.

This conclusion would complete your argument. It does so by evolving yet another assertion from the preceding system of assertions that you have already stated. The next chapter will explain how to build conclusions that develop beyond what they summarize.

Name _____ Instructor_____

Do You Understand the Concepts of Part 3?

The following questions will aid you in summarizing what you have learned in the chapters of Part 3. Try to answer these from memory.

What does a forecast initiate?

When is an argument coherent?

In what way is an expanding sequence more valuable for the writer than a diminishing sequence?

How do you judge whether or not an assertion relates to the context that contains it?

Now Put the Concepts of Part 3 to Use in Your Own Writing

Working through the following writing situations will demonstrate your mastery of this chapter. Your instructor may suggest other situations or may encourage you to create your own.

By using all the concepts you have learned in Part 3, you should be able to evolve a sequence of assertions that constitutes a coherent line of reasoning.

Following are two writing situations. For each of them, perform the following operations:

1. Find five or six assertions related to your subject and write them out as sentences in the spaces provided.

2. Find a tentative organizing idea and write it in the space provided.

3. Select a reader and state the reader's implied question.

4. List the categories of your information.

5. Sequence your categories and your assertions within them (including your organizing idea) to reveal a coherent line of reasoning.

6. Expand each assertion into a paragraph in order to develop a complete argument. Make sure that the first paragraph of the argument forecasts your tentative organizing idea and your plan for developing it.

WRITING SITUATION 1

Suppose you are asked to make a statement about this subject, "the effect of television on young children," at a one-day forum. Your audience will be composed of television programmers, educators, and concerned parents. You do not wish to alienate anyone in your audience, but you do want to make your own organizing idea evident. Take any position on this issue and develop a line of reasoning that supports your organizing idea. You might use any of the following information.

The effect of television on young children has recently become a controversial issue. Those who see television as little threat to young minds argue that television is a harmless amusement. They claim that children are quite capable of differentiating between fantasy and reality. Any effects of television on children, they are convinced, are balanced by home, school, and societal influences.

On the other hand, those who are concerned about the effects of television on young minds argue that children spend a disproportionate amount of time watching television. They are concerned about the amount of violence that children are exposed to on television. They also fear that many programs that children view are too mature in content for young people. The time children spend watching television, they claim, gives children little time to develop their own imaginative powers. They are also convinced that the development of such "basics" as reading and writing are sacrificed to a more passive approach to the world.

Set of Assertions:

1.

2.

3.

Name _____ Instructor_____

4.

5.

6.

Tentative Organizing Idea:

Reader and Reader's Implied Question:

Categories of Information:

_____

_____

_____

_____

_____

_____

Name _____ Instructor_____

Sequence of Assertions (including your tentative organizing idea):

T.O.I. <u>   </u>

   <u>   </u>

   <u>   </u>

   <u>   </u>

   <u>   </u>

   <u>   </u>

   <u>   </u>

Paragraphs:

Paragraphs (continued):

BUILDING AN ARGUMENT

Name _____ Instructor_____

Paragraphs (continued):

BUILDING AN ARGUMENT

You are planning next year's courses, and you wish to take one course of independent study in a subject of your choice. You must write a proposal justifying your project to a committee of faculty members in several different disciplines.

The committee will decide to approve or reject your proposal on the basis of your explanation of the following: (1) what your subject is; (2) what you want to find out about that subject; (3) your focus or principal point of inquiry; (4) how you will go about your inquiry; (5) what kind of evidence you plan to use; (6) how you will know when the project is complete; (7) your proposal title; and, (8) your capability of carrying out the project.

Your statement should acknowledge these eight items, but the items in themselves need not constitute your argument. You are free to combine your information and present it in any order that you wish.

Set of Assertions:

1. my subject is capital punishment

2. I wish to find out what the ~~situation~~ situation involving capital punishment involves and what side of the issue is the side for me.

3. my focus is from The view of A person who knows nothing About cAp. pun. But is wanting To explore The issue so that They can take a stand.

4. Through Research And AnAlysis.

5. Documented evidence out of books written on The situation.

6. when I can honestly say what I feel The Right side of The issue is.

7. what is The Right side of The cApitAl punishment issue?

8. OH 'extremely cApAble.

Tentative Organizing Idea:

Reader and Reader's Implied Question:

Categories of Information:

History

Future

Present Situation

Pro's

Con's

Morality vs Illegality

BUILDING AN ARGUMENT

Name _____ Instructor_____

Sequence of Assertions (including your tentative organizing idea):

T.O.I.

____

____

____

____

____

____

Paragraphs:

Paragraphs (continued):

BUILDING AN ARGUMENT

Name _____ Instructor_____

Paragraphs (continued):

BUILDING AN ARGUMENT

Name _____ Instructor_____

Part 4: Completing the Argument

17. Developing a Conclusion

The chapters of Part 3 introduce the basic principles of sequencing. They describe functional sequences, the uses of forecasting, and the nature of an argument as a system of interrelated assertions. Accordingly, Part 3 emphasizes the evolution of a developed organizing idea: that is, a developed conclusion based on any set of information. The writer forecasts a tentative organizing idea and then refines it into a conclusion. This chapter discusses that final stage in the evolution of an organizing idea.

What Is a Conclusion?

A conclusion is an inference: a decision you make about the significance of interrelated information. You cannot make this decision when you start to write a statement. It becomes increasingly possible only as you write.

You recall that Chapter 13 defined an argument as a system of interrelated assertions. The conclusion of an argument is an assertion that completes the argument. It reflects a developed understanding of the implications of a line of reasoning. It is partly an insight and partly a decision that something reasonably follows from whatever precedes. It is the writer's most developed judgment about the significance of the whole system of assertions.

What are the features of a conclusion? The question can easily be answered with reference to the strictest kind of argument: the syllogism from classical logic. Most lines of reasoning are not as limiting as the syllogism, and very few written statements elaborate that kind of argument. Nevertheless, the syllogism provides a simple example.

One form of the syllogism looks like this:

A is B
C is A
C is B

The first two equations in this model are "premises"; the third equation is a "conclusion." The function of the first two equations is to predict the third. Here is an example of a syllogism: "Human beings are rational; Socrates is a human being; therefore, Socrates is rational.

Notice two interesting facts about the conclusion of this argument. (1) All the information in the conclusion can first be found in the premises, but not in the same relationship that the conclusion establishes. The premises furnish the information from which the conclusion will be derived; they imply the conclusion. (2) Moreover, the conclusion is a new assertion that is not precisely stated at any earlier stage of the argument. That Socrates is rational is the writer's own unique discovery about the significance of the information as it develops from the premises of the argument. The rationality of Socrates is what the writer has come to understand from the implications of this line of reasoning.

The developed conclusion of any argument is not contained in the premises but in the interrelationships among them. A conclusion follows from a system of assertions, but it also extends the significance of that system in some way.

A conclusion is derived from the line of reasoning that precedes it, but it is also a new assertion, a new kind of information that the writer recognizes only by writing. The conclusion is a discovery as well as a summary. This newly discovered assertion may resemble the tentative organizing idea at the beginning of the writer's statement, but it has also progressed and expanded beyond that tentative idea by means of the implications in an evolving line of reasoning.

The conclusion of any argument possesses these characteristics, whether or not it is a syllogism. A syllogism is an argument that arrives at a necessary conclusion using no more than two previous assertions. Most arguments are not this limiting. Any number of assertions may constitute an argument, sometimes many more than the syllogism possesses. Moreover, a variety of conclusions might be possible for a given statement, depending on the interrelationships among assertions along the way. Any evolving argument restricts the writer to certain kinds of conclusions but not to any one conclusion.

Regardless of the type of argument, the conclusion is derived from the chain of assertions that precede it, yet is different from any one of the assertions that gave rise to it. A conclusion is a discovery as well as a summary. Given an assertion A, followed by B, followed by C, followed by D, the developed conclusion represents a gradual recognition that some new assertion X is the one the writer was looking for in the first place.

Recall the illustration from Chapter 15 regarding the crisis in urban education. Using that example, here is the way a developed conclusion can evolve through the implications of a line of reasoning.

The chain of assertions, you will remember, developed in this way:

TENTATIVE ORGANIZING IDEA

The quality of education varies considerably between urban and surburban schools; the causes are complex, and the cure may be difficult to find.

SUBSEQUENT ASSERTIONS

1. Adequate facilities and qualified teachers are provided for children from wealthy homes but not for children from poor homes.

2. Shortcomings in urban schools have often been attributed to lack of funds.

3. Economists support this view.

4. The problem is not merely economic; it runs deep in the American system of values.

5. The schools are a middle-class instrument used to "Americanize" the children who attend them.

6. School boards are dominated by representatives of the middle class.

7. Inner-city children are alienated from the schools. As institutions of the middle class, the schools do not adequately serve the needs of these children.

These assertions imply a range of possible conclusions, but before writing any conclusion, it will be helpful to retrace the writer's line of reasoning.

The writer's tentative organizing idea is his or her best estimate of how the argument is likely to develop. The writer knows that the conclusion will develop from the causes for the inequality of urban and suburban schools, but the causes of their influence on any solution to the problem are not yet clear.

The argument contains seven assertions. The first assertion (about unequal staff and facilities) simply states the case. The writer does not intend to prove this inequality but states a given situation in order to proceed to a discussion of its causes.

The second assertion (about the lack of funding) establishes the cause most commonly associated with the inequality, namely, the distribution of funds. Sensing that this cause is probably superficial, the writer states it early in order to clear away popular misconceptions before dealing with more subtle problems.

The third assertion (the economists' view) gives token support to the second assertion, which the writer will later disqualify.

The fourth assertion (that this is a problem of values) is the turning point in the argument. The writer is now going to analyze the problem and describe what appears to be the deeper causes of educational inequality.

The fifth assertion (schools are a middle-class instrument) equates the school system with a particular system of values. The writer is preparing to argue that this system of values, applied indiscriminately, penalizes urban schools.

The sixth assertion (middle-class dominance of school boards) implies that all the schools serve middle-class interests.

The seventh assertion (the different needs of inner-city students) and the eighth assertion (urban schools do not serve these needs) explain why the schools have alienated inner-city children.

Now for the conclusion. What has really been the writer's purpose? Why elaborate the causes of educational inequality unless you are searching for a solution? The writer looks at the causes in order to come to some conclusion about changing the situation.

A conclusion, remember, has two characteristics. It is implied in the line of reasoning that precedes it, yet it is a new assertion not specified at any earlier point in the argument. What conclusion can the writer draw from the argument developed here? The writer cannot state a particular solution since the argument does not focus on the evaluation of solutions; instead, it stresses what any solution will involve. A simple cause of the problem, such as poor distribution of funds, could be simply removed by reallocating the funds. But the writer has found deeper causes: the biased value system assumed in the schools and the resulting alienation of inner-city children. Such complex causes require a different order of response. Indeed, perhaps no response is possible; perhaps there is no immediately feasible solution, which is precisely the writer's developed conclusion. This conclusion is implied in the chain of reasoning, but it is not expressly stated anywhere in the assertions that anticipated it.

Here is a possible conclusion to this argument. (It happens to be a paragraph, but it could be a sentence, or two paragraphs, or the last chapter of a book: there is no set length to the conclusion of an argument.) Notice that it begins with a summary but ends with a new assertion. Read the last sentence first; then see how it derives from the assertions that precede it.

> The problem we must confront, then, does not involve simply a redistribution of funds, so that the urban schools can improve facilities, hire more staff, or provide better materials for students. The problem goes far deeper. It lies in our attitudes and expectations regarding what the public schools should be and what they ought to do. It concerns the role that schools should play in the development of our children. To solve the problem we must reappraise our traditional understanding of what the role might be. We must realize that what is good for one school may not be good for another. *But unfortunately, because the problem is so intimately tied to a system of values that educational authority takes for granted, a workable solution may be a long time coming.*

Now glance back at Chapter 15 and compare the opening paragraph of the statement on education with the concluding paragraph given here. Can you now see the difference between a forecasted tentative organizing idea and a developed organizing idea? Can you see how the second grows out of the first through the evolution of a system of assertions?

An Illustration of Developing a Conclusion

A system of assertions is listed below. Because it is a system, it exhibits a line of reasoning. Your task is to recognize that line of reasoning, to assess its implications, and then to infer a conclusion that represents your estimate of the significance of the argument that the system conveys. Given this system:

1. Write a concluding assertion in the space provided. (A concluding assertion follows from the implications of the line of reasoning in the system but also extends the significance of that system in some way.)

2. Write a paragraph or two including this assertion as your conclusion about the significance of the argument that the system conveys.

SYSTEM OF ASSERTIONS

TENTATIVE ORGANIZING IDEA

> Forest fires destroy vast areas of timberland yearly, and since that land is the last escape we have from hectic city life, its loss can be measured in very human terms.

ASSERTION

> Forest regions are among the last primitive areas available to most Americans living in the crowded cities.

ASSERTION

> Access to forest regions allows for at least a brief escape from the frustrations of urban life.

ASSERTION

> Forest fires destroy thousands of acres of timberland each year.

ASSERTION

> Many fires are caused by freaks of nature such as lightning.

ASSERTION

> Many fires are also caused by human carelessness.

ASSERTION

If we lose this last retreat from the crowded cities, we could end up forever trapped in them.

CONCLUDING ASSERTION

(which follows from the system but also extends its significance)

We must make every effort to preserve our wilderness from the destruction brought by forest fires; in particular we must eliminate fires that are the result of human carelessness.

CONCLUDING PARAGRAPH(S)

(an expansion of the concluding assertion)

The message is plain. If we are to continue to enjoy the last remaining wilderness areas available to us, we must protect those areas from the massive destruction brought about each year by forest fires. Certainly we should keep up the fire watches so essential to forest preservation during the dry months. But more important, we must guard against the campers and vacationers who annually burn down thousands of acres through their own carelessness. We must protect our forests from their worst enemy— not the forces of nature but the thoughtlessness of man. When we endanger our wilderness retreats, we are endangering one of our last alternatives to the relentless pressures of urban life.

Summary

As you write you refine your tentative organizing idea until it has become a developed organizing idea. When you have evolved a developed organizing idea from your system of assertions, you are ready to write a conclusion to your statement. This conclusion is both a summary and a statement of a new relationship.

Given a successive chain of assertions, you gradually recognize that some new assertion is the one you have been looking for. This new assertion is your developed organizing idea. It follows from your system of assertions, but it extends the significance of these assertions.

Name ————————————— Instructor————————————————

Do You Understand the Concept of Developing a Conclusion?

The following questions will aid you in summarizing what you have learned in this chapter.

What is a conclusion derived from?

The conclusion of an argument is ————————————————— that

follows from a system of —————————————————.

What are the essential features of a conclusion?

Now Develop Some Conclusions of Your Own

Working through the following writing situations will demonstrate your mastery of this chapter. Your instructor may suggest other situations or may encourage you to create your own.

You should be able to write a conclusion to any system of assertions; that conclusion should reflect the evolution of a tentative organizing idea into a developed understanding of the significance of a sequence of assertions.

Two systems of assertions are listed below. Because they are systems, each exhibits a line of reasoning. Your task is to recognize a conclusion that represents your estimate of the significance of the arguments that the two systems convey. For each system of assertions:

1. Write a concluding assertion in the space provided. (A concluding assertion follows from the implications of the line of reasoning in the system but also extends the significance of that system in some way.)

2. Write a paragraph or two including this assertion as your conclusion about the significance of the argument that the system conveys.

SYSTEM OF ASSERTIONS 1

Tentative Organizing Idea:

Although science courses are different from humanities courses in subject matter, method, and purpose, each type has its own unique value in an educational program.

Assertion:

The purpose of education is to multiply perspectives, to expand awareness, to develop the confident humility that results from a flexible outlook and a broad range of interests.

Assertion:

The natural sciences extend our awareness of the physical world around us.

Assertion:

Practical applications of the natural sciences can improve our relation to our environment, affecting the make-up of our world and the quality of our lives.

Assertion:

Courses in the natural sciences can help to develop both technical skills and a self-disciplined, logical approach to discovery of new knowledge.

Assertion:

Humanistic studies—philosophy, literature, history, and the rest—are concerned with our responses to the world around us, our peculiarly human needs, fears, and aspirations, and our peculiarly human ways of expressing them.

Name _____ Instructor_____

Assertion:

> Knowledge gained from the humanities can improve the quality
> of our relations with one another as mutually dependent mem-
> bers of the human family.

Assertion:

> Courses in the humanities help to develop our awareness of the
> spiritual, moral, and aesthetic values that make human life worth-
> while and that distinguish it fundamentally from all other forms
> of life.

Concluding Assertion (which follows from the system but also extends its
significance):

Concluding Paragraph(s) (an expansion of the concluding assertion):

Concluding Paragraph(s) (continued):

COMPLETING THE ARGUMENT

SYSTEM OF ASSERTIONS 2

Tentative Organizing Idea:

The free expression of ideas is essential to any healthy society.

Assertion:

New ideas are disconcerting; they challenge our preconceptions and threaten our settled and comfortable view of the world.

Assertion:

Galileo shook the very foundations of theology when he disputed the validity of the Ptolemaic universe.

Assertion:

There is no question that new ideas can be dangerous to the smooth and orderly running of a state or social institution.

Assertion:

Thomas Paine and others throughout history roused the demon of social unrest and showed the way to bloody civil revolt.

Assertion:

Social progress is almost always painful since it is achieved through the downfall of earlier attitudes, beliefs, and social institutions.

Assertion:

Progress is achieved only through the confrontation of the old and outworn with the new and revitalizing.

Assertion:

Progress assumes the freedom to dissent from established ideas and institutions.

Assertion:

Suppression of dissent is the quickest route to social stagnation and eventual decay.

Concluding Assertion (which follows from the system but also extends its significance):

Concluding Paragraph(s) (an expansion of the concluding assertion):

18. Using Strategic Repetition

The chapters of Parts 3 and 4 have described how to forecast, how to evolve a sequence of assertions, and how to develop a conclusion. These are different operations you perform in developing your tentative organizing idea, yet they are not clearly separated into neat parts or subdivisions of the whole statement. Writing operations are not separable. Instead, they are interrelated and continuous. They interpenetrate to produce the system of relationships that comprises any statement.

A writer continually forecasts throughout the length of any statement, continually reevaluates the significance of information, and repeatedly makes choices about what to say next. Most important, the writer informs the reader of these choices as soon as possible.

What Is Strategic Repetition?

The writer cannot assume that the reader's frame of reference is acknowledged merely by an initial forecast of the opening paragraphs. Instead, through every paragraph of the statement, the writer must reveal to the reader some relationship between what has already been said and what is likely to be said. The writer must continue to forecast what is about to happen with respect to what has already happened.

As you write you can reveal the network of relationships in any system of assertions by a process of strategic repetition; that is, you can use repetition to make an argument visible to your reader. By this means you can expand an argument to its full potential.

Engineers often speak of repetition as "redundancy." The Apollo moon rockets, for example, included redundant systems as a safeguard against breakdowns. For every important system in these rockets a back-up was installed to do exactly the same job if the primary system failed. These systems were redundant, therefore, because they performed the same task.

Redundancy is also a natural feature of language. In speech, if one sound fails to convey its signal, other sounds will back it up. In syntax, if one word fails to convey a significance, the sentence pattern provides other words to reinforce it. Such redundancy enables a listener to understand a message without even hearing it perfectly, as in the case of a bad telephone connection.

Because redundancy is a natural characteristic of language, you can make it work for you in your writing. You can use it to control the development of a tentative organizing idea. Unlike speaking, however, writing requires deliberate and strategic repetition: you intentionally repeat important pieces of information at critical points in an argument. This repetition serves both as a reminder and as a forecast. It creates emphasis by reformulating information, and it shows the reader how what comes next follows reasonably from what has gone before. Strategic repetition shows the reader how the writer intends assertions to be interrelated; therefore, it holds an argument together for the reader.

The writer's strategy of repeating is essential. Repetition is distracting when there is too much or too little of it. More subtly, repetition is unconvincing in either extreme. If it is too literal, it merely calls attention to itself. On the other hand, if it is merely fragmentary, it causes confusion about how the assertions of an argument relate to one another.

The second problem—inadequate repetition—is more common and more serious than the first. In any case, useful repetition depends on the writer's skill in linking assertions. Strategic repetition operates below the reader's consciousness of what is happening in a statement in order to remind the reader of the logical progress of that statement.

What Are the Kinds of Strategic Repetition?

There are two types of strategic repetition, grammatical and logical. Grammatical repetition, which is simpler, entails sentence overlap. It operates on the surface of a statement explicitly to relate one sentence to another, and thereby reduces verbal ambiguities.

Consider this example: "The dragon ate its mother. Then, having dined, it retired to its den." The second sentence overlaps the first in several ways. "Having dined" repeats the verb in the first sentence, though in a different form. The subject of the first sentence, "the dragon," is twice repeated by the two pronouns of the second sentence ("it" and "its"). The new information in the second sentence is that the dragon retired to its den. But the writer provides this new information in the context of the earlier information to show how the dragon's second action is related to the first.

Logical repetition, the second type, occurs in the structure of a statement. It is subtler and more important than sentence overlap because it reveals the logic of a line of reasoning rather than the mere relationship of sentences. Just as sentence overlap is a way of reducing verbal ambiguities, so overlap among the assertions is a way of reducing logical ambiguities. Strategic repetition is a deliberate repetition of concepts that are common to more than one assertion. Such repetition operates deep in an argument; it establishes the logical connections among the assertions. Specifying these connections helps the writer to expand and develop an argument to its logical completeness. To reveal your line of reasoning is to expand your own awareness of your subject.

The simplest example of structural repetition can be drawn from the syllogism. Recall the syllogistic argument you saw in Chapter 17: "Human beings are rational; Socrates is a human being; therefore, Socrates is rational." Suppose, as a reader, you were given only the first and third assertions: "Human beings are rational; therefore, Socrates is rational." Does the argument make sense? Yes, but only if you infer a missing assertion: namely, that Socrates is a human being rather than some other kind of creature.

In a simple and rigorous argument like the syllogism the missing second premise does not cause serious uncertainty: the reader can easily make the leap (which involves a logical inference) from first premise to conclusion. But in a less rigorous argument—more commonly found in written statements—a missing assertion can often cause serious confusion. The reader cannot make the connection between what has come before and what follows. The reader will not see the logical continuity that the argument intends to establish.

To include the second premise in the argument above (that Socrates is a human being) is to provide strategic repetition. Here is why: the second premise repeats some of the information that was found in the first premise; that is, both premises make reference to "human being." The second assertion relates Socrates to the subject of the first assertion. If Socrates is a species of "human being," and if a "human being" is rational, then Socrates must be rational—which is the conclusion of the chain of reasoning. The redundant second premise is not vital to the argument's development because you can safely infer it, but including it gives the reader greater assurance about the writer's logic in moving from the first assertion to the third.

Here is another example, where the repetition plays a more important role in the development of an argument. Assume that the following assertions have been abstracted from a statement and that each assertion represents a paragraph:

1. Children are not born as Democrats or Republicans.

2. A person's parents will often determine whether that person becomes a Democrat or a Republican.

Does the second assertion logically follow from the first? No indeed. It happens to follow in sequence, but it does not logically follow. The second assertion is not yet a consequence of the first. (You can test the logic of any concluding assertion by placing the word "therefore" in front of it to see if it actually follows from the preceding assertions.) In this case there is a gap between these two assertions. Can you see that at least one other assertion (and perhaps more) must occur between them in order to relate them?

Suppose you choose the following assertion to relate these other two:

1a. Children are influenced in their political choices before they are old enough to vote.

Does this assertion establish a logical relationship? Not yet. It is a good start, but only a start. With this assertion you have a possible reason for the fact that children who are not born as Democrats or Republicans nevertheless grow up to become one or the other. That is to say, you have one possible way of linking the two assertions you began with. But there are potentially dozens of reasons for the political consciousness of the maturing individual. What makes "parental influence" all that special? How is the reader to progress from the fact that people join political parties to the supposition that parental influence is the most important reason? The leap is simply too far.

Even with this new assertion (that children are subject to influence) it is difficult to see what relationships the writer might have intended, because there is not yet enough logical overlap in the information. But the writer can strengthen the argument by expanding it and by incorporating a greater degree of structural repetition. The writer can shorten the logical leaps by making more assertions, for example:

1b. Most children grow up under the supervision of their parents.

1c. Attitudes of children often resemble those of their parents.

1d. Children tend to be influenced politically as well as in other ways by their parents.

Given these assertions, it is possible to conclude that: "Therefore, a person's parents can determine his or her choice of party." This at least would be an arguable case for the importance of parental influence on the development of political consciousness, whether or not a reader might agree with it. More to the point, the writer has revealed a coherent line of reasoning by shortening the leaps from one assertion to the next.

This set of assertions could be organized in several ways. Here is one way:

1. Children are not born as Democrats or Republicans.
   1a. Children are influenced in their political choices before they are old enough to vote.
      1b. Most children grow up under the supervision of their parents.
      1c. Attitudes of children often resemble those of their parents.
      1d. Children tend to be influenced politically as well as in other ways by their parents.

2. A person's parents will often determine whether he or she becomes a Democrat or a Republican.

Notice the amount of repetition in all the assertions. For example, 1b, 1c, and 1d are related by the fact that parents are in a unique position to influence the behavior of their children. There is also new information in each assertion: (1b) children are supervised by their parents; (1c) children are prone to have the same attitudes as their parents; (1d) children can be politically influenced by their parents. But the new information is conveyed in each case by means of a logical overlap with information that the reader has already received. At every point in the developing argument you can see how what has gone before relates to, and anticipates, what is to come next. This repetition enables you to see at the same time how the argument is evolving.

If you were to expand each of these assertions into a new paragraph (such as you have done in earlier chapters), you would expand the entire statement from the original two paragraphs to a new total of six. It is not the increase in words, however, that makes an argument complete. Rather, it is the chain of assertions—with no logical gaps—that completes it. Strategic repetition enables you to say everything you want to say. You expand an argument by repeating concepts that have occurred in previous assertions. A concept worth repeating may have been stated or implied, but in any case you perceive it as being common to more than one assertion. By this means you specify a reasoning process and thereby complete your statement.

An Illustration of Strategic Repetiton

The argument given below is a syllogistic argument in which the middle assertion (the second premise) is missing. Given the two assertions, A and C, your task is to furnish a third assertion, B, that will relate A to C through repetition. Then expand each assertion into a paragraph in order to develop a complete written statement.

ASSERTION A

The enforcement of laws is essential to social order and to the protection of our civil rights.

ASSERTION B

ASSERTION C

Police forces, therefore, are essential to social order and to the protection of our civil rights.

In order to derive assertion B you must assess the implications of the two assertions you began with. What have they in common? How can you move logically from A to C? You do it by making explicit the implications you see in the association of A and C. If the writer is arguing that police forces are essential, then he or she must be implying the fact that police forces are agencies of law enforcement—and probably the most effective agencies. Hence:

ASSERTION B

Police forces are the most effective agencies of law enforcement.

EXPANSION OF THE ARGUMENT

ASSERTION A

Few would argue with the assumption that obedience to civil authority is essential both to the orderly running of a society and to the protection of its individual citizens. And most of us are also aware that some individuals willfully choose not to obey civil authority, and in so doing endanger the lives and rights of others. Without the law, and without some effective means of enforcing the law, antisocial individuals would be free to violate the rights of other citizens without fear of punishment. Law enforcement, therefore, is a vital element of any social institution insofar as it prevents and penalizes violations of the civil order.

ASSERTION B

The most effective organ of civil law enforcement is the police force. That force is responsible for preserving the social order and for safeguarding the rights of citizens. Other types of law enforcement—ranging from individual retaliation (an eye for an eye) to vigilante justice—have proven ineffective in promoting "the greatest good for the greatest number." In these forms of enforcement, punishment is arbitrary and not subject to firm enough control. In addition, the enforcement is not broad or fair enough in its application; it is motivated by self-interest rather than the interest of the society as a whole. Only the organized and well-trained police force, always subject to the control of the citizenry, can provide an effective means of enforcing the law.

ASSERTION C

It is clear, therefore, in spite of the popular arguments to the contrary, that police forces are vital to the preservation of social order and the protection of the rights of society's individual members. Certainly, there have been abuses of police power, and certainly the bad policeman poses as serious a threat to our civil rights as any criminal. But this only suggests the importance of defining and restricting the powers and responsibilities of any police force so that such a force truly answers to the interests of the society it is designed to serve. Proposals simply to abolish police agencies fail to consider the social realities and human failings that have made necessary the very institution of law. If we need law, and if we have found no more efficient an agency for its enforcement than the civil police, then evidently we must continue to maintain our police forces as the best safeguard of our social order.

Summary

As a writer you cannot assume that your initial forecast will sufficiently acknowledge your reader's frame of reference. You must continue to forecast throughout the length of your statement. By continuing to forecast you reveal to your reader some relationship between what you have already said and what you are likely to say as you continue your statement.

You can reveal the network of relationships in any system of assertions by the process of strategic repetition. There are two kinds of strategic repetition: grammatical repetition, which explicitly relates one sentence to another, and logical repetition, which reveals implicit connections between assertions in a line of reasoning. As you specify the connections you are making by the process of strategic repetition, you expand your own awareness of your subject.

Do You Understand the Concept of Strategic Repetition?

The following questions will aid you in summarizing what you have learned in this chapter.

In addition to making an initial forecast, what else must the writer do in order to acknowledge the reader's frame of reference?

How does the writer reveal to a reader the network of relationships in a system of assertions?

How does intentional repetition of important pieces of information at critical points in an argument help your reader follow your line of reasoning?

What are the two types of repetition?

What does strategic repetition reveal to your reader?

Now Use the Concept of Strategic Repetition in Your Own Writing

Working through the following writing situations will demonstrate your mastery of this chapter. Your instructor may suggest other situations or may encourage you to create your own.

You should be able to use repetition as a means of revealing the logical development of an argument to your intended reader in functional writing situations.

Two syllogistic arguments are given below. But in each case the middle assertion (the second premise) is missing. For each argument, given the two assertions, A and C, your task is to furnish a third assertion, B, that will relate A to C through strategic repetition. Then expand each assertion into a paragraph in order to develop a complete written statement.

WRITING SITUATION 1

Assertion A:

   The crisis of our cities can be solved only with help from the federal government.

Assertion B:

Assertion C:

Solving the urban crisis will involve fighting through a lot of red tape.

Paragraphs:

COMPLETING THE ARGUMENT

Name _____ Instructor_____

Paragraphs (continued):

Paragraphs (continued):

Assertion A:

In a truly free society, women deserve to have the same rights and privileges as men.

Assertion B:

Assertion C:

The United States is obliged to insure that women receive the same rights and privileges as men.

COMPLETING THE ARGUMENT

Name _____ Instructor_____

Paragraphs:

Paragraphs (continued):

COMPLETING THE ARGUMENT

Name _____ Instructor_____

Paragraphs (continued):

The arguments below are not syllogistic arguments; that is, more than one assertion must occur between the given assertions in each case if the argument is to make sense. For each of these arguments, your task is to furnish as many assertions as necessary between the two given assertions in order to relate the first one to the last. (You should provide no less than three new assertions and no more than four.) Then choose one of these arguments and expand each assertion into a paragraph in order to develop a complete written statement.

First Assertion:

Noise levels in centers of dense population have reached intolerable proportions.

Next Assertion:

Next Assertion:

Next Assertion:

Next Assertion:

Last Assertion:

It is essential that we alter the approach patterns of commercial jets.

SET OF ASSERTIONS 2
First Assertion:

A sense of values is important to the mental health of any individual.

Next Assertion:

Next Assertion:

Next Assertion:

Next Assertion:

Last Assertion:

A society is only as strong as its spiritual convictions.

SET OF ASSERTIONS 3
First Assertion:

Workers in foreign countries are often more industrious and enterprising than workers in our own country.

Next Assertion:

Next Assertion:

Next Assertion:

Next Assertion:

Last Assertion:

The U.S. government should restrict the quantity of foreign mer-
chandise coming into the United States.

Expansion of any one of these arguments:

Name _____ Instructor_____

Expansion of any one of these arguments (continued):

Expansion of any one of these arguments (continued):

COMPLETING THE ARGUMENT

Name _____ Instructor_____

Expansion of any one of these arguments (continued):

19. A Functional Writing Model

Chapter 19 is the culmination of your work in this course. Mastering it depends on your grasp of everything that has preceded it. For the first time, in this chapter, you will have a chance to integrate all the concepts and operations you have learned earlier, making them work for you as a unified and extended process.

What Is the Functional Writing Model?

Earlier chapters have indicated that writing is not a mechanical succession of separate operations. Instead, it is a unified process of organizing and evaluating information. This process involves the writer in repeated decisions about forecasting, sequencing, and concluding. When you write, the decisions you make in the opening paragraph of a statement are the same kind of decisions you make in the last paragraph. You do not merely start with a forecast, then evolve a sequence of assertions, then develop a conclusion. Forecasting is a way of concluding; sequencing is a way of forecasting; concluding is a way of relating successive forecasts in order to show the significance of a sequence.

Decisions about forecasting, sequencing, and developing a conclusion are all interrelated. The whole process of making these interrelationships can be described as the Functional Writing Model. This model is simply a representation of the continuity of the concepts and operations described in earlier chapters. Like any model, it is an ideal form.

The model represents the writing process: it does not predict what any given statement may look like.

The primary characteristic of the Functional Writing Model is the continuous interdependent relationship that exists between the writer and the reader. Your reader will have to cope with every decision you make about your information. By focusing on the reader you insure that your developing statement will indeed communicate the information you intend in precisely the way you intend it.

Focusing on the reader has an even subtler value. The reader is far more deeply involved in your own process of discovery than you might think. Focusing on the needs of a reader primarily helps you. The reader's need to be kept informed of what you are doing can actually help you to discover the significance of what you want to say. In other words, you depend on the reader to guide your own systematic progress toward a fully developed conclusion that you were unaware of when you began to write. Remember the Contract Theory of Writing: it is easier to organize your information for somebody else than it is to organize it for yourself.

How Does the Functional Writing Model Help the Writer?

The chapters of Parts 3 and 4 have indicated how the interdependence of writer and reader works. The three operations described in these chapters—forecasting, sequencing, and concluding—are the basic features of the Functional Writing Model. These operations help you even more than they help the reader. This is how:

1. *Forecasting.* You invert your own natural learning process and forecast a tentative organizing idea, thereby presenting your best guess about the importance of your information. You continue to do so throughout your statement. This helps the reader to cope with your selection and arrangement of the assertions to come. More profoundly, the forecast provides you with a sense of the task you have set for yourself; it clarifies in your own mind the limits of your subject and the most effective means of dealing with that subject. Hence, you have helped yourself by helping your reader.

2. *Sequencing.* As you evolve your system of assertions, you continue to forecast what is about to occur with respect to what has already occurred. You do this chiefly through strategic repetition. Your inclusion of overlapping assertions helps the reader to keep track of your line of reasoning. More to the point, it helps you to discover the logical connections you wish to make as you move from one assertion to the next. Again, you help yourself by helping your reader.

3. *Concluding.* As you evolve your system of assertions, you grow more certain of the nature of your developed conclusion. Once you have perceived the essence of that conclusion, you begin to write about it: you tell the reader what it is. This helps the reader to appreciate the significance of your line of reasoning, but even more, it helps you to discover a new kind of knowledge about your subject, a new assertion which you were unaware of when you began to write. By recalling your obligation to show the reader the value of your developed statement, you specify that value more clearly for yourself. In other words, you help yourself by helping your reader.

This mutually beneficial relationship between you and your reader can be expressed in terms of a visual scheme. Remember the two pyramids in Chapter 11, representing the different learning processes of the writer and the reader:

Reader's learning process: *Writer's learning process:*

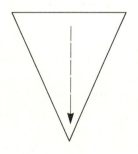
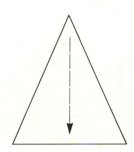

The reader's pyramid signifies a learning process that moves from conclusion to detail. Accordingly, it describes a diminishing sequence (as in a news story).

The writer's pyramid also signifies a learning process. But this process is the discovering of new significance by means of making and relating assertions. When you write, therefore, you naturally evolve an expanding sequence.

In the extreme, these two learning processes are mutually exclusive. They are at odds with each other, which is the usual dilemma of functional writing: how can you, as writer, learn something new about your subject and still accommodate your reader's need to know what you have not yet discovered?

The Functional Writing Model solves this dilemma. It enables you to relate your assertions by the very process of helping the reader to anticipate their significance. The Functional Writing Model represents the solution in this way: it incorporates both pyramids (the reader's priorities and the writer's learning process) by superimposing the reader's priorities on the writer's learning process:

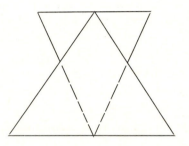

Here is the significance of the Functional Writing Model. You begin with the reader's priorities in order to get started. The hardest part of writing is getting started, but focusing on the reader overcomes this difficulty. You use the reader's implied question as a point of departure. You begin your statement by estimating what you need to find out and what its importance will be. This way of beginning gives the reader a reason to keep reading. More important, it gives you a way to keep writing.

You should not be exclusively concerned with the needs of your reader. In fact, you should be primarily concerned with your own process of discovery, with your own movement from a tentative organizing idea to a developed conclusion. The Functional Writing Model shows how this movement can be simplified by looking to the reader for help. According to the model, you provide your reader with a tentative organizing idea so that the reader can discover the ultimate significance of your information. By acknowledging the reader's implied question in your search, through every phase of that search, you help yourself to cope with the complexities of your information.

Look again at the Functional Writing Model and notice the bonus that it offers you:

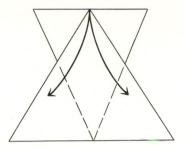

The bottom base line is longer than the top. The base of the writer's pyramid, where you ultimately arrive, is broader than the base of the (inverted) reader's pyramid where you started. The broader base of the writer's pyramid represents the bonus of a conclusion that you did not anticipate when you began to write.

By anticipating assertions for the reader as you go along, you learn new relationships within your subject that expand your earlier understanding and may go significantly beyond it. You evolve your new understanding by the very process of accommodating your reader's implied question. You reveal to the reader every new discovery you make through each phase of your evolving statement until you finally recognize your conclusion. Your process of continual summary and forecast actually causes you to see the expanding significance of your own line of reasoning.

Recognizing the implications of the Functional Writing Model makes writing quicker and easier. The model shows you how to get started. Then it shows you how to make appropriate choices as you write. Finally, it shows you that your conclusion will naturally outgrow your initial forecast.

Illustrate the Functional Writing Model by Yourself

You can build your own illustration of the concept of the Functional Writing Model. You can do so by choosing any extended statement you have already written and converting it to an abstract (or summary) using the operations of the Functional Writing Model. Specifically, you can forecast and sequence what you have already written, and you can identify the conclusion you have already reached.

To convert your original statement you will first have to analyze it; that is, you must first identify the assertions that you will then restructure in your summary. Later in this chapter you will have a chance to do this.

When you have completed the abstract or summary, you will be able to see the structure of the original statement. You will also be able to see how the Functional Writing Model can guide you in expanding and developing that statement to its full potential—perhaps even to a new conclusion that was inherent in your original structure.

Summary

Decisions about forecasting, sequencing, and developing a conclusion are all continuous and interactive. For any written statement, the sum of these decisions, or the process of making these relationships, can be described as the Functional Writing Model. The primary characteristic of this model is the continuous interdependent relationship between writer and reader.

As you use the three operations described in Parts 3 and 4, forecasting, sequencing, and concluding, you become more aware of how this interdependence works. Forecasting for your reader helps you to clarify the limits of your subject, sequencing for your reader helps you discover the logical connections among assertions that you are making, and concluding for your reader helps you to see more clearly the value of your developed statement.

Do You Understand the Concept of the Functional Writing Model?

The following questions will aid you in summarizing what you have learned in this chapter.

What is the primary characteristic of the Functional Writing Model?

Explain how forecasting helps both the reader and the writer.

Explain how strategic repetition helps both the reader and the writer.

Explain how developing a conclusion helps both the reader and the writer.

Explain the significance of the broader base of the writer's pyramid in the Functional Writing Model.

Now Use the Functional Writing Model in Your Own Writing

Working through the following writing situation will demonstrate your mastery of this chapter. Your instructor may suggest other situations or may encourage you to create your own.

You should be able to use the Functional Writing Model in any circumstance that requires you to write a functional statement.

What follows is an exercise in condensation. It is valuable in several respects. First, the ability to summarize is often required in functional writing situations, particularly when space and time are short and only the most crucial information is relevant. Composing an abstract of some extended statement you have already written will help you to develop such a skill.

Second, the ability to go to the heart of an issue is a prerequisite to clear thinking and to clear writing. It can save you time and effort, especially when you are confronted with copious material or a complex subject. Writing the abstract will give you some practice in isolating key ideas and issues relevant to a subject with which you are already familiar.

Third, writing the abstract will give you a personal illustration of the Functional Writing Model. Your task is to summarize the longest statement you have written in connection with this book. If you can do that successfully, you will be able to see the essential structure of the argument you have developed. You will see the logic of the argument and possibly the extent to which that argument is not yet developed. Most important, you may see its implications for entirely new lines of reasoning that had not occurred to you before.

For the longest statement you have written in this course:

1. List the most critical assertions on which your argument depends; you should include no less than three but no more than six; write them down in the space provided.

2. Write an abstract (that is, a comprehensive summary) of 400 to 700 words, using your knowledge of the Functional Writing Model; this abstract should include the principal features of your system of assertions, the ways in which your assertions interrelate, and your conclusion (that is, the significance of the system as you see it).

NOTE: "Using the Functional Writing Model" means using what you know about forecasting, sequencing, and concluding in order to guide both you and your reader through your statement.

Most important assertions:

1.

2.

3.

Name _____ Instructor_____

4.

5.

6.

Paragraphs:

COMPLETING THE ARGUMENT

Name _____ Instructor_____

Paragraphs (continued):

Paragraphs (continued):

COMPLETING THE ARGUMENT

Name _____ Instructor_____

Paragraphs (continued):

Paragraphs (continued):

Name _____ Instructor_____

Paragraphs (continued):

Paragraphs (continued):

COMPLETING THE ARGUMENT

20. Review of the Text

This chapter will serve as a practical review of the concepts you worked with in Part 4: developing a conclusion, revealing an argument through strategic repetition, and organizing by means of the Functional Writing Model. Chapter 20 is also designed to provide a study guide for the final examination in the course. The examination will be described presently. Before you read that description, however, here is a review of the concepts of Part 4, so that you will be able to use them as you write.

What Has Part 4 Indicated about Writing?

Above all, the development of any statement entails a sustained reciprocal relationship between the writer and the reader. Specifically, the writer uses the reader's implied question continuously as a guide for developing an organizing idea. From the forecast to the conclusion, a writer evolves an argument by anticipating the reader's need to see how the tentative organizing idea is evolving.

Both writer and reader benefit from this relationship, but the writer benefits more. The benefit to the reader is ease of reading, but the benefit to the writer is a broader, richer awareness of the significance of the information about the subject.

These chapters have described several concepts that define the nature of development in any functional writing situation. You know how to overlap successive assertions in order to reveal your line of reasoning to your intended reader, and you know how to develop a conclusion based on the implications of the line of reasoning you have evolved.

The Three Essential Concepts of Part 4

The **conclusion** of an argument is a final assertion that reflects a developed understanding of the implications of a line of reasoning. It is partly an insight and partly a decision that something reasonably follows from whatever has come before.

The conclusion of an argument represents the writer's final judgment about the significance of a given system of assertions. It is the outcome of that system. As such, the conclusion is a new assertion that is implicit in the system itself but not specifically stated in any earlier assertion. It logically follows from the system, but it also extends the significance of that system in some way. A conclusion, therefore, is a discovery as well as a summary. It is derived from the implications of a given system of assertions, but it is different from any one of the assertions that anticipated it.

Strategic repetition is the intentional and controlled restatement of important pieces of information at critical points in an argument. Such repetition establishes the coherence of the argument in two ways:

a. It reinforces critical information to help the reader remember what the writer considers most important.

b. It shows the reader how successive assertions interrelate by clarifying what the assertions have in common and by revealing how one follows plausibly from another.

Repetition makes the reader conscious of the sequential logic of the writer's statement. It establishes logical connections among the assertions that constitute the writer's argument.

The **functional writing model** is an ideal form that represents the writer's unified and coordinated process of developing any statement. Writing is not a mechanical succession of separate activities but a fully unified process of organizing and evaluating information. A writer does not merely start with a forecast, then evolve a sequence of assertions, then develop a conclusion. On the contrary, forecasting is a way of concluding; sequencing is a way of forecasting; concluding is a way of relating successive forecasts in order to show the significance of a sequence. The Functional Writing Model shows how these three activities occur as a continuous, integrated process.

The model explains the writer's decisions about forecasting, sequencing, and concluding in terms of the same essential characteristic: namely, the interdependent relationship that exists between the writer and the intended reader. You help your reader primarily in order to help yourself.

a. You forecast the significance of your assertions so that your reader can cope with their arrangement and sequence. But by this process of forecasting, you also locate the significance more clearly for yourself.

b. You provide strategic repetition so that your reader can keep track of your evolving sequence of assertions. But in providing this repetition, you also reveal for yourself the logical connections you wish to establish among your assertions.

c. In developing a conclusion, you help your reader to comprehend your line of reasoning. More important, this process of concluding increases your own awareness of your subject by revealing a new assertion which you had not been aware of when you began to write.

In each of your decisions, therefore—about forecasting, sequencing, and concluding—you help yourself by helping your reader. You use your reader's implied question as a guide to expanding your own knowledge of your subject.

Recognizing the implications of the Functional Writing Model makes writing quicker and easier. The model shows you how to get started (by forecasting your tentative organizing idea). Then it shows you how to make appropriate choices as you write (both in the selection and the arrangement of assertions). Finally, it shows you how your conclusion provides a new kind of knowledge about your subject (that is, a new assertion representing the completion of your process of learning the significance of your information).

Do You Understand the Concepts of Part 4?

The following questions will aid in summarizing what you have reviewed in this chapter. You should try to answer them from memory.

Explain how the conclusion of an argument follows from a line of reasoning but also adds something to it.

What is the value of strategic repetition in the development of a sequence of assertions?

According to the Functional Writing Model, how does the writer profit more than the reader from developing a statement according to the reader's implied question?

Now Prepare for the Final Examination

You should be able to complete a final examination on all of the concepts that are described in the chapters of this book.

The final examination will serve as a cumulative review of all the concepts and their uses, as presented in Chapters 1 through 20. As part of your examination you will be asked to write a statement of 500 words describing the theory of functional writing that the course has elaborated. Your reader will be the Common Reader.

You may write this statement in two phases. The first phase will consist of your answers to a set of questions about the essential characteristics of the process of functional writing. Each answer will be a sentence. Together your answers will be a set of assertions.

The second part of the examination will entail your writing a statement that incorporates as its assertions the set of answers you derived in the first part. Basically, in this statement, you will be asked to describe the relationship between a writer, the subject, and the reader.

It is expected that your statement will follow the Functional Writing Model: it should include a forecast of your tentative organizing idea, a sequence that accommodates the needs of your intended reader, an adequate degree of strategic repetition, and a developed conclusion.

Some Review Questions to Aid in Your Preparation

Briefly review Chapters 6, 10, 16, and 20. Then attempt to answer the review questions listed below.

These questions are designed to help you in preparing for the final examination. The questions appearing on the first part of the examination will be similar to the questions presented here. You have already answered many of these questions in earlier chapters. Therefore, you need not repeat the extensive answers you may have provided in the chapters from which the questions are taken. Instead, you should try to answer the questions briefly (a sentence or two at most) in order to facilitate your review of relevant information.

Notice that each question includes a reference to an earlier chapter or chapters in which the appropriate response can be found. You need not look at earlier chapters for answers until you have written a response to each question. Answer the question as well as you can; then check your answer.

QUESTIONS

1. In what sense is writing a learning process for the writer? (Chapter 2)

2. Why is a subject of so little help to the writer? (Chapter 2)

3. What is an assertion? (Chapter 2)

4. Where does an organizing idea come from, and what does it do? (Chapter 3)

COMPLETING THE ARGUMENT

5. Why should an organizing idea be thought of as a sentence and not merely as a word or phrase? (Chapter 2, Chapter 3)

6. When is an assertion an organizing idea? (Chapter 3)

7. Why do different writers discover different organizing ideas in the same set of information? (Chapter 4)

8. What is the difference between a frame of reference and an organizing idea? (Chapter 4)

9. What distinguishes evidence from information? (Chapter 5)

10. What questions can you ask to determine whether a piece of information will be good evidence? (Chapter 5)

11. Compare the function of a subject with the function of an organizing idea. Which is more helpful in relating pieces of information? (Chapter 6)

12. What basic fact does the writer need to recognize about the intended reader's frame of reference? (Chapter 7)

13. What does focusing on a reader entail? (Chapter 7)

14. State the five traits of the Common Reader. (Chapter 8)

15. Explain specifically how focusing on the five traits of the Common
    Reader helps you select and organize what you want to say.
    (Chapter 8)
    a. Trait 1:

b. Trait 2:

c. Traits 3, 4, 5:

16. State two reasons why a writer must focus the tentative organizing idea on the intended reader's frame of reference. (Chapter 8)

17. What is functional evidence? (Chapter 9)

18. Compare the order in which the writer and the reader normally learn the significance of the information in a statement. (Chapter 11)

19. How can the writer's sequence of information accommodate the reader's implied question? (Chapter 11)

20. What two things must a writer forecast to the reader early in the developing statement? (Chapter 12)

21. What is an argument? (Chapter 13)

22. What is the function of an assertion in an argument? (Chapter 13)

23. Why is an expanding sequence of assertions preferable to a diminishing sequence? (Chapter 14)

24. How do you forecast an expanding sequence? (Chapter 14)

25. When is an argument coherent? (Chapter 15)

26. If an argument is a system of assertions, what is the conclusion of an argument? (Chapter 17)

27. What are the two characteristics of any conclusion? (Chapter 17)

28. How does the writer reveal to the reader the network of relation-ships in any system of assertions? (Chapter 18)

29. How does intentional repetition of important pieces of information at critical points in an argument help your reader follow your line of reasoning? (Chapter 18)

30. What is the primary characteristic of the Functional Writing Model? (Chapter 19)

31. Explain how forecasting helps the reader and the writer. (Chapter 19)

32. Explain how strategic repetition helps both the reader and the writer. (Chapter 19)

33. Explain how developing a conclusion helps both the reader and the writer. (Chapter 19)

Index